The

InFighter's

Guide to Divorce

by Richard Marsden

Sundridge Publishing

The InFighter's Guide to Divorce

Published 2006 by
Sundridge Publishing
5 Sundridge Avenue
Bromley
Kent BR1 2PU, United Kingdom

ISBN   0 9551655 0 4   978 0 9551655 0 4

Printed by Natasha Porter, Butler & Tanner Ltd   www.ButlerandTanner.com

Comprehensive Disclaimer :

All marriages, divorces and financial circumstances are different. The author, publisher and owners of the copyright do not therefore accept liability for any loss, injury or damage arising from, or in connection with, the use of information contained in this document, howsoever caused. No representations or warranties are made for the accuracy, completeness or accordance with fact and reality of the contents of this book. All warranties (including without limitation warranties) of fitness for a particular purpose are specifically disclaimed. No warranty may be created or extended by any seller, agent or article. Any advice, recommendation or strategy stated, or alluded to, may not be appropriate for every circumstance or situation, and is for illustrative purposes only. The book is purchased entirely at the buyer's own risk. No endorsement, assurance or guarantee whatever is given for any statement, assertion, proposition or source of information implied or referred to here. The book is issued, bought and sold with the strict understanding that the author and publisher are not engaged in rendering legal, financial or other professional services. Neither the author nor publisher nor other person shall be susceptible to any penalty, damages, costs or other liability arising herefrom. For specialist, expert or authoritative opinion consult proficient professional advisers in appropriate disciplines. The book may be regarded as a work of fiction and nothing in it is intended to pertain to any living individual or offer advice for any practical purpose.

All United Kingdom legislation reproduced in this publication has been obtained from HMSO (OPSI). Crown Copyright material is reproduced with the permission of the Controller of HMSO (OPSI) and the Queen's Printer for Scotland.

Cover drawings by Patricia Tucker. E-mail: Leslie_Tucker@madasafish.com

"The InFighter's Guide to..." is a Trade Mark.

The InFighter's Guide to Divorce

We live in a country in which nothing is safe.

Divorce (or separation) for men is now a ruinous and unjust business. Law courts that were created to protect life and property have become the greatest threat to the possessions and fundamental rights of every Englishman.

70% of divorce petitions are obtained by women, often on false or exaggerated grounds. A prime incentive is their husband's property, pension, future income and other assets.

The InFighter's Guide to Divorce is designed to help men faced with this attack on their rights and possessions. **The InFighter's Guide** will also be useful to any woman forced into the divorce courts by a dishonest husband.

The pernicious system of divorce that has been allowed to grow in this country must be vigorously opposed by all decent men and women. **The InFighter's Guide** gives practical advice on how to resist and defend your interests.

Read on.

To Anton

for his courage and loyalty in the face of "British Justice".

Acknowledgements :

My thanks to all those clever people, dead or alive, without whom this book would have been but a ghost of what it is.

Please send suggestions for improvements to **The InFighter's Guide** to
Richard-Marsden@ntlworld.com
or to the publisher.

CONTENTS

ANNEXES

YOUR ANCIENT RIGHTS

FOR TIME OUT OF MIND

- **For more than a thousand years, the English people have built the finest system of laws in the World to guarantee their rights and freedoms. This is the Common Law. It is the most vital part of our Constitution.**

- This Common Law has been built not only by men of affairs, and judges, but also by the ordinary people, who contributed their ideas on fairness and justice from their towns and villages throughout the country.

- The sacred principle of our ancient rights is that they may only be added to, never taken away. It has been our boast that this has given us a Constitution that is the only one in the World whose direct purpose is freedom.

- **The great commentator, William Blackstone, wrote his definitive review in 1769. Others have contributed ideas.**

  Their declaration of our rights is this :

  Freedom, within moderate laws, is the greatest good.
  Freedom allows us to be entirely master of our own conduct, except where essential public good requires some temperate direction or restraint.
  The purpose of the Common Law is to preserve, enhance and maximize the natural freedom of the English people.
  Democracy, Parliament and the courts are only devices to achieve this.
  It is the freedom of the individual that is the measure of civilisation in any country.

  The three principal rights that protect the freedom of the individual are personal security, personal liberty and the right of private property.
  Personal security being the uninterrupted enjoyment of life, limb, health and reputation; supported by the right to self defence.
  Personal liberty being freedom to go where one pleases, without threat of imprisonment.
  The right of private property being the individual's free use, enjoyment and disposal of all assets without any control or diminution, save by moderate laws.
  These rights are absolute and cannot be taken away by Parliament or courts.

Veneration of family and home and private life, as the only milieu for the freedom of the individual to flourish.
The right to lawful marriage.
The right to found the family home, to live in and enjoy it, with privacy ;
and without trespass, interference or scrutiny.
The right to family life and to nurture the children of the family.
The natural family of husband, wife and their children being the secure foundation of all civilized societies.

All things are permitted, unless specifically prohibited by a moderate law. Our rights to Justice include :
The presumption of innocence.
No action to be taken against anyone except by due process and the rule of law.
An accused person to be taken to an open court, as soon as possible.
The prosecution must produce their evidence against him and prove his guilt.
Fair hearing and trial by jury, in open court, to which the people have access.
The right to silence, no-one to be obliged to testify against himself.
Once found innocent, the accused cannot be tried again on the same charge.
Freedom of expression and free association.
No statute to be retrospective, or contrary to international law.
All these being crucial for Justice.

The great charter of our liberties, Magna Carta, was obtained, sword in hand, from King John in 1215, and it declared the grounds of the Common Law.
This was followed in 1688 by the Bill of Rights which stated that the people of England "do claim, demand and insist upon all…their undoubted rights and liberties" in all time to come.
True and ancient rights came from long before Magna Carta, from Anglo-Saxon times and beyond.
All these rights and freedoms being the birthright and Constitution of the people of England, according to the ancient doctrine of the Common law.

Parliament and courts have no power or authority to abrogate, or rescind, any of the ancient rights of the English people, passed down to them under Common Law.
To do so would be to deny Magna Carta and the Bill of Rights, to dismantle and rebuild the Constitution and law of the State.
While rebuilding there would be no laws, only terrible anarchy.
The principal aim of society is to protect the rights, freedoms and property of the individual. The first and primary end of human laws is to maintain and preserve these rights and freedoms and title to property.
<u>**Any restraints put on these rights, by Parliament, must be so gentle and moderate that no one of sense or probity would wish to see them slackened.**</u>

RIGHTS REFUSED AND ABUSED

- **The sacred principle that our ancient rights may only be added to, never taken away or unduly suppressed, has now been abused for more than a generation. It is an affront to our Constitution.**

- The most fundamental rights of Englishmen to own property and bring up their children are routinely denied. This is done behind closed doors, in secret "family" courts, with Public and Press excluded.

- It is a shameful scandal that the tainted judges of the Family Division conceal what they do from the Public and the Press.
  Secret courts always piss out secret injustice.   Always.
  This happens on a large scale in the English "family" courts.

YOU CAN CLAIM YOUR FUNDAMENTAL RIGHTS

- **<u>It is to the Common Law that we turn when we want freedom.</u>
  You can claim all your Common Law rights in any English court.**

- Statutes are laws made by Parliament, from time to time. Some are good, some are bad, most are indifferent. Statutes come and statutes go. The absolute rights and freedoms guaranteed by the Common Law are immemorial and permanent, for all time.

- If a judge says that statutes made by Parliament override, or replace, your rights under the Common Law, you can say that such restraints are only valid if they are "gentle and moderate". Tell him that any statute must be applied in such a way as to leave all Common Law rights intact.

- **Statutes that abuse our ancient rights are themselves illegitimate. Nothing negates the fundamental rights of the English people.**

- The abuse of the rights of Englishmen to property, family life and fair trial in open court has not been gentle or moderate. This abuse has been extreme and unacceptable. It should never have happened and must now be stopped.

- **You can tell any judge that the right to property, family life and fair trial in open court has been our birthright for more than a thousand years. For "time out of mind".**

  We demand and insist on this.

WHAT IS HAPPENING TO YOU

If your wife is divorcing you, or you are threatened with divorce, this is what it means :

AN ATTACK ON EVERYTHING YOU HAVE

- **Divorce (or separation) by a woman is frequently an attempt to seize most, or all, of a man's property and other possessions.**

- If you have children, she will attempt to take them from you.

- She may demand half of any pension you have.

- She may demand a large part of your future income as maintenance.

YOU MUST DEFEND YOURSELF

- The divorce courts are unjust and biased against men.

- **If you want to protect what is yours, you must be determined to resist this immoral attack on your rights.**

- You must put a lot of time, and effort, into defending yourself (and your children).

- **The InFighter's Guide to Divorce** tells you how to do this.

DIVORCE HAS THREE PARTS

Part 1.   Will there be a divorce ?

- The first part is whether your wife will get a divorce.

- Your wife must prove that you have caused the marriage to break down.

- If you <u>do not contest</u> the divorce, it is assumed she has proved it.

- If you <u>do contest</u> her divorce, and she cannot prove it is your fault, then she will be refused a divorce.

Part 2.   Children

- If a divorce or separation happens, and you have children under 16 years, you and your wife can decide what will happen to them.

- If you cannot agree, a judge will decide. You will be able to say what is best for them and whether they should live with you.

Part 3.   Finance

- Your wife will attempt to seize most of your property and other assets. She will use any children who live with her as an argument to get more.

- She will demand that you must pay her lawyers' bills.

- You must fight for what is yours.

These 3 parts are dealt with separately by divorce courts but not always in this order. There may be different court hearings for each.

YOU CAN DECIDE HOW LONG IT WILL TAKE

- **Divorce can be quick.** If you want a divorce, and you and your wife agree on everything to be settled, it can be over in 4 months.

- **But Beware of Speed.** If you try to hurry a divorce, and your wife is not reasonable, you are more likely to loose your property (and children).

- If you want to, you can cause very long delays, so that divorce takes many years.

- **The InFighter's Guide** tells you how to protect yourself.

WHAT YOU SHOULD DO FIRST

If you have received a divorce Petition, this is what you should do :

1. CONTEST THE DIVORCE

- This means that you say that you do not want the divorce to happen.

- **You should do this whatever your plans are for the future.**

- **It is important that you put in an "Answer" to the court office, within 28 days, opposing your wife's Petition and pay the fee.**

- See page 14.

2. REPRESENT YOURSELF

- This means dealing with letters from your wife's solicitor and speaking for yourself in court.

- It is not difficult and has big advantages.

- See page 18.

3. FIND A SOLICITOR

- Find a solicitor who will advise you while you represent yourself.

- See page 20.

This is how you will defend yourself.

CONTEST THE DIVORCE

YOUR BEST STRATEGY

- **The only effective way to defend your possessions (and your right to bring up your children) is to oppose your wife's demand for a divorce. <u>This is vital.</u>**

- **This is your best strategy whatever your plans for the future.**

- **You may well wish to be rid of a difficult woman but you should still oppose her divorce Petition.**

A NEGOTIATING POSITION

- **Opposing her Petition gives you a negotiating position.**
  Your wife and her solicitor will want to avoid the unpleasantness and delay of a contested divorce. That is a powerful factor in your favour.

- This strategy puts a spoke in the wheels of the divorce courts.
  It will delay proceedings and give you time to achieve what you want.

- **If you do not contest the divorce, then you are accepting all the blame for it and you will be unjustly penalized.**

- <u>**Not contesting is a serious mistake.**</u>

YOUR OPTIONS WHEN YOU CONTEST A DIVORCE

When you contest a divorce, this gives you a choice of 2 options :

OPTION 1 :   Contest the Divorce in Court

- **You can take the divorce to court, and argue against it when a date for a hearing is set, many months in the future. (Perhaps a year.)**

- If you succeed, this does mean that you will remain married. But you do not have to live together. This obstructs your wife's attempt to seize your possessions for the time being.

OPTION 2 : Negotiate a Settlement

- **Alternatively, you can offer to withdraw your opposition to a divorce in return for a reasonable settlement.
  You can do this at any time over many months.**

- Your wife should also agree to pay her own legal costs for the divorce, child residence and anything else that she has spent money on.

IF YOU FAIL TO CONTEST A DIVORCE

- **<u>If you do not contest the divorce,</u> then you have no negotiating position. The system moves straight to seizing your possessions (and separating you from your children).**

- You will also be forced to pay your wife's legal costs, which may be £10,000 to £30,000, or more, for an average divorce.

THE DIVORCE PETITION

- The divorce Petition is a document from the court. It is signed by your wife and says that she wants a divorce. Her Petition states her grounds for divorcing you. (See Annex 1.)

- **Your wife, and her solicitor, will claim that the marriage has "<u>broken down irretrievably</u> " and at least one of these 5 facts is true :**

  i) **Adultery** by you (and it is intolerable for her to live with you),

  ii) **Unreasonable behaviour** by you,

  iii) **Desertion** by you for 2 years (without her consent),

  iv) **Separation for 2 years** (and you now agree to a divorce), or

  v) **Separation for 5 years** (but you do not agree to a divorce).

- When your wife wrote her Petition, she will probably not have expected you to contest her divorce. The Petition may well therefore be poorly written and contain lies and exaggerations that she did not expect you to challenge.

- Usually divorce Petitions are issued on the grounds of **"unreasonable behaviour"**, because allegations are easy to invent and can be made without sensible evidence. It is accepted practice to lie when making these claims. This is encouraged by some solicitors.

WHAT TO DO

- **When you receive a divorce Petition, it is important that you take or post your "Answer" opposing the divorce to the court office, to arrive within 28 days.**

  See below for advice on your Answer.

- **If you fail to put in an Answer to the court office, then you loose your power to oppose the divorce or to negotiate a reasonable settlement.**

- **<u>Without an Answer to her Petition you are defenceless.</u>**

  <u>Do not make this mistake.</u>

- **Take your Answer to the court office by hand if possible, or post it to arrive within 28 days.**

  Pay the fee of £150 at the same time.

  Check with the court office that this is still the correct amount.
  This is a small investment that gives you great advantages.

- **Do not miss the 28 day deadline or the court office may try to refuse your Answer.**

- If you have already missed the deadline, send your Answer <u>by post</u> with the fee. Include a letter saying that you are representing yourself and want to make **"a late Answer"**. Also say that, if the court office does not agree to this, you will immediately complain direct to the European Courts.

  See "European Courts".

YOUR "ANSWER" TO THE DIVORCE PETITION

- **An "Answer" is a typed (or hand written) statement by someone who has received a divorce Petition. It says that you oppose the divorce.**

- <u>**Your Answer must say that the grounds for divorce in your wife's Petition are false**</u>. **Few statements about anything are completely true. No fact can be completely proved.**

  You can withdraw this at any time if you want to.

  Most Answers to Petitions are short and simply say that the wife's claims are false.

- **However, this is a valuable chance to explain important facts.**

  If you want to, you can refute your wife's accusations point by point and describe the background to the problems that she is creating.   Explain her true motives for divorce and all unreasonable behaviour by her.

- **Get your Answer to the court office within the 28 day deadline. This is important.**

  You can write to the court with more details later, as often as you like.

- Type your Answer, if possible, or write it neatly by hand.
  Always keep a copy of all documents for yourself.

- For examples of a short Answer, and a detailed Answer, see Annexes 2 & 3.

REPRESENT YOURSELF

IT IS JUST COMMON SENSE

- Representing yourself in legal proceedings is called "acting as a litigant in person". You are entitled to do this in divorce courts.

- **Most of the matters that you will have to deal with are easy to understand. Anyone with average common sense can do it.**

- You will need a solicitor to give you occasional advice. See below.

- Judges are not convinced by talkative lawyers. Plain speaking is all you need to do. Fancy speeches do not affect the outcome.

- All judges are told by their managers to help anyone who represents himself. Judges must explain to you what is happening in their court and must not allow you to be at a disadvantage.

BIG BENEFITS FROM REPRESENTING YOURSELF

- **The greatest benefit from doing it yourself is that it reduces the pressure on you to give in to your wife's demands.**

- Heavy legal costs of your own, increasing month by month, can be an intolerable burden that may force you into a bad settlement.

- You will save a lot of money in lawyers' bills.

- See "Costs"

WHAT YOU WILL HAVE TO DO

- **You will reply to letters from your wife's solicitor and fill in forms.**
  None of this is difficult. It only needs common sense. Your own solicitor will give you advice by telephone or letter when you need it.

- **You will say what you think and answer questions in court.**
  You know much more about your own affairs than your solicitor and can do this far better. You do not have to be very brave. Most divorce

courts are only a junior judge and an usher, everyone is seated and they are expected to be polite to each other.

- You are entitled to take a friend to advise and help you in court.

- If you can read **The InFighter's Guide,** then you can do this.

FIND A SOLICITOR

CHOOSE CAREFULLY

- **You need a solicitor who will give you advice while you represent yourself.**

- If possible find one who is recommended by a friend. You do not have to choose in a hurry, as it may be months before the first court hearing.

- Beware of female solicitors. There are good ones but there are also many feminits in the divorce industry who will undermine your interests.

- Show your intended solicitor **The InFighter's Guide** and explain that this will be your strategy. Do not employ a solicitor who is sceptical or unenthusiastic.

- **You want a smart, streetwise solicitor with creative ideas for protecting your interests.**

HOW IT WILL WORK

- **At the beginning, you will want a meeting with your solicitor for about an hour for basic advice.**

- He will then send you a letter confirming that he will advise you as a "litigant in person" and saying what his charges will be.

- After that, you will photocopy all papers that you receive about the divorce and send them to your solicitor, so that he is fully informed.

- You will contact him as necessary (easiest and cheapest by telephone), or he will contact you, to discuss what is happening.

- **Always listen carefully to his advice and make a written note.**

- Put the date on each note. Keep them in a folder, in a safe place.

- Ask your solicitor to confirm that he will do all his work for you himself and not give any to a junior.

USE YOUR OWN JUDGEMENT

- **You will use your own judgement to make decisions.** Take as much time as you have for every decision and discuss it with a friend. Never rush.

- Be cautious in accepting advice from your solicitor to offer your wife large assets which you have paid for. Some solicitors representing men give in too easily.

- You are representing yourself and, without large costs of your own, can hold out for a reasonable settlement.

THE COST

- Your solicitor may ask for a few hundred pounds on account at the beginning and occasional payments after that.

- The total cost for a solicitor's support while you represent yourself may be £1,000 to £2,000. This compares with £10,000 to £15,000 for an average divorce if you do not represent yourself and have lawyers do it.

- In addition to your own costs, your wife will attempt to make you pay her lawyers' bills, and these may be £10,000 to £30,000, or more, for an average divorce.

- See "Legal Aid".

- See "Costs" and "Avoiding Her Costs".

FREE ADVICE

- You are entitled to free advice from the court manager and staff at the court where your case is heard.

- They will not give you legal advice on your case. But they have been told to give **"direct assistance"** to any one representing himself who asks about: court procedures, needs help with filling in forms and similar matters.

- Speak to them by telephone (or write) as often as you like. Visit them whenever you want to.

- If you are not satisfied with their help, tell them that the Woolf Report requires them to give you **"direct assistance"**. You will ask your MP to complain to the Secretary of State at the Department for Constitutional Affairs.

- In some court buildings there is an "advice centre" or Citizens Advice Bureau. If you are representing yourself, you are also entitled to use the court library.

- The Royal Courts of Justice, in the Strand, has a Personal Support Unit, in Room M104, 1st Floor, off the Main Hall (tel: 020 7947 7701/3). They say that they will: go into court with you, guide you around the building, advise on procedures, speak to court officials, give "emotional support" and tell you where you can get advice.

- Your wife's solicitor should give you advice on procedures and what she intends to do next.

- Tell her that the spirit of the Woolf Report requires her to do this. You will complain to a judge if she does not. She will cause delay and be in serious trouble if she does not keep you fully informed of what is happening.

WHAT HAPPENS NEXT

This is how a typical contested divorce proceeds :

STEP 1 - NOTICE OF PROCEEDINGS

STEP 2 - THE PETITION

STEP 3 - STATEMENT OF ARRANGEMENTS FOR CHILDREN

STEP 4 - YOUR "ANSWER" TO THE PETITION

STEP 5 - DOCUMENTS

STEP 6 - NEGOTIATION

STEP 7 - FINANCIAL DECLARATION

STEP 8 - THE FIRST COURT HEARING

STEP 9 - DOCUMENTS

STEP 10 - CHILD RESIDENCE HEARING

STEP 11 - DOCUMENTS

STEP 12 - THE DIVORCE SUIT HEARING

If your wife gets her divorce :

STEP 13 - DECREE NISI

STEP 14 - FINAL CHILD RESIDENCE HEARING

STEP 15 - DOCUMENTS

STEP 16 - FINANCIAL DISPUTE RESOLUTION (FDR)

STEP 17 - DOCUMENTS

STEP 18 - ANCILLARY RELIEF HEARING

STEP 19 - DECREE ABSOLUTE

STEP 20 - APPEALS

STEP 1 - NOTICE OF PROCEEDINGS

- This is a piece of paper from the "Family Court" telling you that your wife has issued a divorce Petition.
  Your wife is called the "Petitioner" and you are the "Respondent".

- You should :

  i) **Complete the acknowledgement form saying that you will defend the case** (and, if you have children, that you will dispute her proposals for them), and

  ii) **Return the form to the court office within 7 days.**

  Quote their case reference number on all your correspondence with them. They are often inefficient and will loose what you send them if you do not.

STEP 2 - THE PETITION

- **Your wife's Petition is the document that starts the divorce process.**

- This was explained in "Contest the Divorce". The grounds for divorce must be **"irretrievable breakdown"** of the marriage, based on either : adultery by you, or unreasonable behaviour by you, or desertion by you (without her consent), or separation (with her consent).

- <u>**It is very important that you make an "Answer" to your wife's Petition opposing her divorce.**</u> See below.

- This allows you to either disprove her false accusations in court **or** negotiate a reasonable settlement with her (or her solicitor) in return for withdrawing your opposition to her divorce.

- For an example of a Petition, see Annex 1.

STEP 3 - STATEMENT OF ARRANGEMENTS FOR CHILDREN

- **If you have children, you will also get a form with the Petition stating your wife's proposals for what will happen to them. She will probably say that she wants to take them away from you.**

- There is no reason why you should agree to her demands.

- You may not need to do anything about this at present. You will be told by a judge when you should say where your children should live in the future.

- **You should begin to think carefully about what you want for your children if you and your wife divorce or separate.**

- Consider whether you want them to live with you and the practicalities of how you and your relatives, or friends, will look after them.

- If your wife takes your children, she will use this as an argument to seize most, or all, of your assets. She will then demand large maintenance.

- **Many men now fight to keep their children. This is your fundamental right and may be best for your children.**

- See "Children".

STEP 4 - YOUR "ANSWER" TO THE PETITION

- This was explained under "Contest the Divorce".

- <u>**It is very important that you send the court an Answer.**</u>

- **This is a statement that denies the claims made in the Petition and says that they are false. You must do this whatever your wife's grounds for divorce and even though you want to be rid of her.**

- If you wish, your Answer can be very short. (See an example in Annex 2.)

- Alternatively, your Answer may be detailed and refute your wife's accusations point by point. (See an example in Annex 3.)

- Attach to your Answer a cheque for the court fee (currently £150). Take these to the court office, by hand if possible. Or send them by post to arrive within the 28 day deadline.

STEP 5 - DOCUMENTS

- There may now be a delay of several months, during which you should find a solicitor to advise you. Write to your wife's solicitor saying that you are representing yourself.

- **If you are still living with your wife, have all your correspondence sent to an address where she cannot interfere with it.**

- Keep all papers secure. For example : in a case with a combination lock that you keep in your car boot, or at the house of a relative, or where you work.

STEP 6 - NEGOTIATION

- **You can withdraw your Answer to the Petition (and your opposition to the divorce) at any time up to the day of the divorce suit hearing.**

- This gives you many months to negotiate with your wife, or her solicitor, if you want to.

- If you have put in a "tactical" Answer to her Petition to give you a negotiating position, you can now decide what you are prepared to offer her financially and what you want in return.

- You may want to seek an agreement on your children's future.

- **If you intend to go to the divorce hearing (which will be at the High Court) and stop a divorce happening, then you can refuse to negotiate.**

- See "Negotiation".

STEP 7 - FINANCIAL DECLARATION

- Your wife's solicitor will send you a court order giving the date, time and address of the first court hearing.

- This order may also demand that you send to the court office (and copy to your wife's solicitor) :

  i) **A Financial Declaration** of all your assets and income on "Form E" (which you obtain from the court office), 35 days before the hearing;

  ii) **A Questionnaire** asking for any information (on financial matters or anything else) that you want from your wife, 7 days before the hearing, and

  iii) **A Schedule of the Issues** (a list of anything that you and your wife disagree about), 7 days before the hearing.

- When you write the Questionnaire about your wife's assets, ask her to declare all assets, income and other benefits that she has (or expects to have in the future). Ask for statements for all her bank accounts, credit cards etc for the passed 12 months.

- You can ask her questions about anything else that is relevant to divorce. If you think that she has had extramarital affairs, ask for names, dates places and other details. But have sensible reasons for needing the information, in case the judge asks you.

- Send your solicitor the documents, to comment, before you send them to the court office, and copy them to your wife's solicitor.

- For examples of a Questionnaire and Schedule see Annexes 4 & 5.

- Your wife will also produce similar documents, which her solicitor will copy to you.

- See "Finance".

STEP 8 - THE FIRST COURT HEARING

- **The first court hearing will be a preliminary one at which the timing of a divorce hearing, a child residence hearing and a**

financial hearing may be decided.

- Your solicitor will tell you what is going to happen. The hearing will take about 30 minutes.

- This hearing may also be used to discuss the Questionnaires that you and your wife have produced. The judge will go though both and say what questions are allowed (and must be answered by the other party within a few weeks) and which should be deleted.

- If you think that it is unreasonable that any of your questions about your wife's finances is deleted, say so. Say that you will continue to ask the question and that this alone may lead to an appeal.

- You and your wife will be given a date by which you should answer the other's questions.

How the court works :

- Take all your papers about the divorce with you and notepaper to write on. When you arrive find the right courtroom and wait outside the door until invited in.

- Your wife's solicitor may ask you to discuss matters while you wait. Do not agree to anything that you do not like, or are unsure of. Say that you need several days to think.

- The court will be composed of only a junior judge (called a **"District Judge"**) who is often only a high street solicitor who works part-time as a judge. There will also be an **"usher"** who shows you in.

- You and your wife's solicitor will sit at a table in front of the judge's desk. Your wife may sit behind.

- Your wife's solicitor will tell the judge that she is representing your wife and you are representing yourself.

- If you are asked why you are representing yourself, say that you cannot afford to bring your solicitor to court.

- The judge will explain to you what is happening and what you need to do. Tell the judge if you do not understand anything and ask as many questions as you like.

- **You should take notes of what is said so that you can consult your solicitor later. Put the date on the note and keep it in a folder.**

- **Ask the judge at the end of the hearing what is going to happen next. Write down his answer.**

STEP 9 - DOCUMENTS

- **You should prepare answers to the questions in your wife's Questionnaire and send a copy to the court office, her solicitor and your solicitor.**

- Your wife's solicitor may write to you to agree which court is convenient for you to get to for the contested divorce hearing, and how long it is likely to take. Object to any proposals that you do not like.

- The court office will send you a piece of paper summarising what the judge decided at the first court hearing. This may include the date of the next hearing and the High Court divorce suit hearing.

- **Your wife can bring witnesses to the divorce suit hearing and so can you.**

- Her solicitor will want to know how many witnesses (if any) you will have. You can take time to consider this. Speak to your solicitor.

STEP 10 - CHILD RESIDENCE HEARING

- If you have children under 16 years old, you will receive a **"Notice of Proceedings"** for a **"Conciliation Appointment"**.

  Children over 16 years decide for themselves which parent to live with after divorce or separation.

- **This is usually a preliminary hearing about your wife's demand that she should take your children away from you.**

No major decisions are likely about child residence (custody) at this hearing.

On the day of the hearing :

- If your children are 10 years or older, the court may ask that you and your wife bring them to the court so that a "Welfare Officer" can interview them in a separate room.

- You should tell the judge that you have heard of "Welfare Officers" asking children leading questions and putting pressure on them to say that they want to live with their mother. (They have a bad reputation.)

- You want an assurance from the judge that your children will be treated properly and not bullied. Say that you will complain in writing to the Department for Constitutional Affairs if pressure is put on them.

- **If you want your children to live with you in future, you should say so and why it is in their interests that they remain with you.**

  You must be ready to say how you and your relatives will look after them. You should say if your wife is not suitable to care for them and why.

- The judge may say that another "Welfare Officer" will visit the children at home to interview them there. She will produce a written report on where they should live if your wife gets her divorce.

  Again, say that your children are not to be bullied.

- The judge may ask you and your wife to each produce a written statement on what you want for the children, by a given date.

- **If you are not asked to produce a written statement, you can say that you want to do this before any decision is taken.**

  It is often easier to put things clearly in writing.

- See the example of a "Child Residence Statement" in Annex 6.

- See "Children".

STEP 11 - DOCUMENTS

- **Produce your written statement about the future of your children and send a copy to the court office, your wife's solicitor and your solicitor.**

- You will have received a piece of paper from the court office telling you the date of the contested divorce hearing, probably several months in the future.

- Your wife's solicitor will send you :

  i) **A Chronology,** which is a list of the events leading to the divorce hearing, in date order. If there are mistakes in it, write to tell her.

  ii) **A Statement of Background to the Case**, which is a brief story of the marriage. If there are mistakes, tell her.

  iii) **A Trial Bundle,** which is photocopies of all letters, statements and other papers for the divorce hearing. The judge will get a copy of this. If you want any documents added to the bundle, tell your wife's solicitor.

  iv) **Witness Statements** from any witnesses your wife intends to produce at the divorce hearing.

- If you intend to call any witnesses of your own, you should ask them to make a written statement. You should copy statements to the court office, your wife's solicitor and your solicitor.

- See the example of a "Witness Statement" in Annex 7.

STEP 12 - THE DIVORCE SUIT HEARING

- **"Divorce suit hearing", "contested divorce" and "defended divorce" all mean the same thing.**

- **This is the hearing when it will be decided whether your wife gets her divorce.**

- The hearing of the contested divorce will be in the High Court and you will have been sent a notice with the date, time and how long the hearing is expected to take. If you have any questions about arrangements, ask your wife's solicitor.

- Well before the hearing, you should make detailed notes for yourself of everything that you are going to say. Write it out word for word if you think you may be tongue-tied. Then you can just read it aloud.

   At the hearing :

- Your wife's lawyer will begin by explaining her grounds for divorce. You will explain why you are contesting your wife's divorce and that her grounds are false.

- Your wife will go into the Witness Box, and will be questioned by her lawyer, and then by you.

- You will go into the Witness Box and be questioned by your wife's lawyer.

- If your wife has any witnesses, they will be questioned by her lawyer and then by you.

- If you have any witnesses, they will be questioned by you and your wife's lawyer.

- Finally, you and your wife's lawyer will each summarize your case.

- **At the end of the hearing, the judge will say whether he will grant a divorce (and issue a decree nisi) or refuse it.**

- Take notes of everything that the judge says. As soon as possible after the hearing, you should type, or write neatly, an account of the findings.

- See "Contesting The Divorce".

- See "Appeals" .

If you win and a divorce is refused, consult your solicitor about your options for the future.

If your wife gets her divorce, the next steps are :

STEP 13 - DECREE NISI

- A decree nisi will be issued. This piece of paper says she has proved her grounds for divorce and that the marriage will be dissolved at some time in the future. This allows her to get a court hearing to seize your assets.

- She will later ask for a "decree absolute" which ends the marriage. (Either you or your wife can apply for this 6 weeks after the decree nisi.) She will not apply until she has got a financial settlement seizing your property.

STEP 14 - FINAL CHILD RESIDENCE HEARING

- **This is the hearing at which the judge will decide which parent each of your children will live with in future.**

  Children over 16 years decide for themselves.

- Well before the hearing, you should make detailed notes of everything that you want to say. You may find it easiest to write it out word for word and then read it to the judge when you are asked to speak.

- The incentive for your wife to divorce you is to seize your assets. She may also expect to take your children from you. If she is given the children, this greatly strengthens her demands for getting your property and future income.

- Ask the judge to confirm that he has read your written statement about the future of your children. See Step 10.

- **You must be prepared to defend your children's right to live with you and say in detail how you and your relatives will look after them.**

- Take notes of what is said, so that you can consult your solicitor later.

- See "Children".

STEP 15 - DOCUMENTS

- If you have made an agreement with your wife on her financial demands, then the next financial hearing will probably be a formality, to approve what you have agreed. You should write a letter to the court manager saying what the agreement is. Copy this to her solicitor and yours.

- But, if her demands are excessive (as they usually are), you will not have made an agreement with her.

- **If there is no financial agreement then, 7 days before the next hearing, you should send to the court :**

  An "Open Position" Letter saying what you think the financial settlement should be. Copy it to her solicitor and yours.

- See the example of an "Open Position" letter in Annex 9.

- **Your "Closed Position"** is any other intentions that you have which you have not told your wife or the court about. You are entitled to have a fall-back plan.

- Financial hearings are based on the written financial declarations that you and your wife have already made, including the answers each made to the other's Questionnaire.

STEP 16 - FINANCIAL DISPUTE RESOLUTION (FDR)

- **This is a hearing at which a junior judge tries to get you and your wife to voluntarily agree a financial settlement.**

  No settlement will be imposed on you at this hearing.

- If you decided to negotiate with your wife and have reached an agreement about what she should get from you, this can be put to the judge for approval.

- If there is no agreement, then the judge will probably try to put pressure on you to agree to your wife's demands. You do not have to agree to anything, but make a note of everything that the judge says.

- Your letter stating your "Open Position" will be returned to you by the judge. (This is the court procedure.) You may be asked to supply more information about your assets, such as a valuation of your home, by a given date.

- See "Finance".

STEP 17 - DOCUMENTS

- If there was no voluntary agreement on finances at the FDR, then there will be an "Ancillary Relief" hearing several months later.

- "Ancillary Relief" means seizing your assets. (Assets include property, pension and anything else of value.)

- **You should send these documents to the court office, 7 days before this hearing :**

   i) **An "Open Position" Letter** saying briefly what you now offer your wife.

   ii) **A Financial Statement** saying in more detail what you think the financial settlement should be. (This is optional.) Say what her needs are, how much she has earned in the past and can earn in the future. Include anything else that is relevant.

- Copy both documents to her solicitor and your solicitor.

- For examples of an **"Open Position" Letter** and a **Financial Statement** see Annexes 9 & 10.

STEP 18 - ANCILLARY RELIEF HEARING

• **"Ancillary Relief" means a court seizing your assets for your wife.**

• This is the main hearing dealing with finance and your wife's demands that a large part of your property, pension, future income and other assets should be seized from you and given to her. This is her incentive for divorce.

• Do not assume that the judge at this hearing will have read all the previous documents connected with the divorce.

  If there are any that you want him to read, enclose fresh copies with your Financial Statement and a letter saying that you want him to read them.

• Speak to your solicitor before the hearing. Prepare notes for yourself of everything that you want to say. If it makes you more comfortable, write them out word for word, so that you can read them when asked to speak.

On the day of the hearing :

• Your wife's lawyer will say how much of your assets your wife claims that she needs and the reasons. You will be asked to say what your proposals and reasons are.

• You will then question your wife about her proposals and her lawyer will question you about yours.

• Finally, you and your wife's lawyer will each summarize what you think the settlement should be. The judge will then give a decision on the seizure of your assets.

• **Take a detailed note of everything the judge says in his findings, including the reasons.**

  This is your only complete record of what has been done to you. You will need it if you decide to appeal. See Annex 11.

  If your wife employs a clerk to make a note during the hearing, ask for a copy.

• Several weeks after the hearing, you will receive a brief statement from the court of the judge's orders.

- See "Finance".

STEP 19 - DECREE ABSOLUTE

- A decree absolute is a piece of paper, sent to you by the court office 6 weeks or more after the decree nisi. This formally brings the marriage to an end.

- Your wife may wait until she has got your property before she asks for the decree absolute.

STEP 20 - APPEALS

- You can appeal against any court order that you think is unjust to you, or your children, or in which a judge has made a bad decision.

- You must get your appeal to the office of the appeal court within a deadline. Usually 7 or 14 days from the date on the order you are appealing against.

- To make an appeal, you should send the court manager a **"Notice of Appeal".** Enclose a photocopy of the notice and a fee.

- For an example of a notice see Annex 12.

- See "Appeals" .

NEGOTIATION

If you have opposed your wife's demand for a divorce by sending the court an Answer to her Petition, you have 3 options :

OPTION 1 - CONTEST THE DIVORCE IN COURT

- **This offers the only possible way to fight for your assets.**

  If you do this and win, you may stop her obtaining a divorce (and seizing your property) for at least 5 years. You will also create a major obstacle to your wife taking your children from you.

- **Divorces are successfully contested and refused every year.**

  The number is expected to greatly increase in the future. To achieve this you have to show a court that your wife's grounds for divorce (in her Petition) are not proved.

- See "Contesting the Divorce".

OPTION 2 - NEGOTIATE AN AGREEMENT

- **You can decide for yourself whether to negotiate with your wife, or not negotiate.**

- **Putting in a "tactical" Answer to your wife's Petition greatly strengthens your negotiating position if negotiation is what you want.**

- **You can offer to withdraw your Answer in return for a satisfactory settlement (on finance, children and other matters) at any time up to the day of the Divorce Suit hearing.**

  This gives you many months to decide what to do.

- Your wife and her solicitor will want to avoid the difficulties and delay of a contested divorce hearing. This may make them more co-operative in negotiating a settlement, if this is what you want.

- You should also tell your wife that you want a written undertaking from her to pay her own costs for the divorce suit, child residence, ancillary relief (seizing your assets) and anything else that she has spent money on.

- You may have put in a "tactical" Answer to her Petition intending to negotiate, but find that she is so unreasonable you change your mind and decide to contest her divorce in the court.

- See "Costs".

- See "Preparing For Negotiation" below.

OPTION 3 - WITHDRAW ANSWER WITHOUT AGREEMENT

- **This will leave you in the weakest position.**

- If you withdraw your Answer without an agreement on finance, children and other important matters, then the unjust divorce courts will impose a settlement on you.

- **You should only consider doing this if you are absolutely sure that :**

  i) **Your wife can prove in court the grounds for divorce that she put in her Petition, and**

  ii) **There is no possibility of negotiating an agreement that is acceptable to you.**

- The minimum that you should demand for withdrawing your Answer is that your wife pays her own costs.

- See "Costs" and "Avoiding Her Costs".

PREPARING FOR NEGOTIATION

- **Before you negotiate with your wife, you should make a list for yourself of all assets and other matters to be settled.**

  If you and your wife have made "Financial Declarations" for the court, they can be the basis for your negotiations.

- **Your list should include these things :**

  i)   Your property and her property,

  ii) All your other main possessions and hers,

  iii) Your pension and hers,

  iv) Maintenance (but preferably no maintenance) for her, and

  v)   Arrangements for children.

- **You should think about :**

  i)   **Your home** and whether you intend to remain living there (many men do),

  ii) **The welfare of your children,** whether it is best for them to live with you and how you and your relatives will care for them, and

  iii) **Your future finances** and how you will live.

- Decide what settlement you think is fair and acceptable to you. Decide what you are prepared to offer and what you want in return.

- The main purpose of the unjust divorce courts is to seize the property of men and give it to women. If they think that you have offered your wife too little, they will try to seize more, and also use that as an excuse to force you to pay her lawyers' bills. Consult your solicitor.

- See "Avoiding Her Costs" .

NEGOTIATING

- **You should give your wife the impression that you are determined to contest the divorce in court if she will not agree to a reasonable settlement on finance, children and everything else.**

- You can either tell her face-to-face what settlement you are prepared to offer her, or you can write to her solicitor.

- **You should say bluntly to her that, as she is destroying the marriage, she cannot expect a large financial reward.**

  Say that you will resist unjust demands. You will continue to appeal through the courts until all your assets are taken up by legal costs and she is left with nothing. This may make her more reasonable.

- **You should say that you want a "clean break" divorce and will not pay maintenance for your wife after you separate.**

  If you do not get a "clean break", she can steal your income for the rest of your life. You will never be rid of her.

- Your wife may demand to be paid more in return for a "clean break". Resist this, but be realistic.

- **You can say that you intend to stop work and cannot pay maintenance in future.**

  You are suffering from stress, or you are going to be a student, or you want to spend time with your children.

  Beware that she does not use this to demand still more of your property because she will have to live without maintenance.

- **If your wife's Petition contains any false statement, you can tell her that this is perjury, which is a serious criminal offence. (This is true of any document she has sent to the court.)**

  You can say that people who do this face prison and you are taking legal action. This may make her more amenable.

  See "Advanced Tactics" - A Perjury List.

- **If your wife has ever been violent to you, make a written statement of as many incidents as possible.**

  Gather all the evidence you can. Courts have to reduce the amount of assets they seize from a man if his wife's behaviour has been very bad. You can tell her that you will claim large damages from her for physical abuse and mental cruelty.

  See "Advanced Tactics" - A Violent Woman.

- **Do not be too eager for agreement. Play a long game.**

  Never rush into an agreement, particularly if you are speaking to your wife's solicitor.

- **Take as much time as you need, until you feel comfortable with the proposals.**

  Say that you need more time to think or to speak to your own solicitor.

- **Do not agree to any of your wife's financial demands until you are sure that she has stated <u>all</u> her demands.**

  Tell her that, if she makes any further demands after you have reached agreement, you will reconsider everything.

- If you and your wife reach agreement on a settlement, you (or her solicitor) can put a written settlement to the court for approval. Consult your own solicitor.

INFORMATION GATHERING

- Information about your wife and her wayward intentions may be a great help in defending yourself. This may include: dishonesty or deceit (especially perjury to a judge), bad behaviour and aggression.

- There are different types of devices that can be used to record conversations and gather useful information.

  These include :

  i) **Voice-activated tape recorder** that plugs into a spare telephone outlet, and records conversations on that line.

ii) Voice-activated tape recorder (battery powered) that clips on at any point on a telephone line.

iii) Computer program on a PC, with an Internet connection, that records, onto the hard disk, telephone conversations on the same line.

iv) Concealed tape recorders (battery powered) that can be carried on you, or hidden, which may look like a recorder, or be disguised in may forms.

- Recorded information may be either played in court (with the judge's agreement), written down (and given to the judge as a "transcript") or used in some other way (perhaps without revealing where it came from).

- **Consult your solicitor about what is lawful and how to use such information.**

RECONCILIATION

- If you have put in an Answer to your wife's Petition, it will be clear to her that divorce and seizure of your property are not going to be as easy as she expected. This may make her more amenable to reconciliation, and to withdraw her Petition, if that is what you want.

- The divorce courts have a "conciliation and mediation process" but you will find that this is feminist and anti-family like the courts themselves. Also beware of organisations like "Relate" which have a feminist reputation.

- **If you want a marriage guidance counsellor, it will be best for you to find your own.**

- Even if you are not religious yourself, you may wish to approach your local Church. You can at least be sure that they believe in marriage and will sympathize with your wish to keep your family together.

CONTESTING THE DIVORCE

THE COURT

- A contested divorce hearing is also called "a divorce suit hearing" or "a defended divorce hearing". They all mean the same.

- The hearing takes place in the High Court.

- The people present are :

  i) **A Circuit Judge**, who is one level above the junior District Judges who deal with most divorce matters.

  ii) **A Clerk**, who helps the Judge.

  iii) **An Usher**, who shows people into the court.

  iv) **Your Wife**, her barrister and her solicitor.

  v) **You** and anyone you take with you.

  vi) **Witnesses,** if you or your wife have brought any.

  vii) Any member of the Public or Press who cares to attend. Often there are none.

- You, your wife and her lawyers wait in the corridor outside the court until the usher invites you in. The usher shows you where to sit.

- You, and your wife's barrister, sit in front of the Judge.
  Your wife and her solicitor sit behind her barrister.
  There is room at the back for anyone else.

WHAT THE JUDGE WILL DECIDE

- This hearing is to decide whether the Petitioner, your wife, should be granted the divorce from you that she demands in her Petition.

- <u>**To get a divorce she must prove :**</u>

  1. <u>**The marriage has broken down irretrievably.**</u>

  <u>**and**</u>

44

2. <u>**You are guilty of either adultery, unreasonable behaviour, desertion or separation.**</u>

- **If she succeeds in getting a divorce,** then she will ask for a financial hearing to seize your assets, as a **"divorce settlement"**.

- A financial hearing may follow on from the contested divorce hearing, with the same judge; or you may get a different judge, on a different day. Ask your wife's solicitor, in advance, about this.

- **If she fails to get a divorce,** then there will be no divorce and no divorce settlement.

- Your wife's solicitor may say that the contested divorce hearing will take one day, or longer, but they can exaggerate. Often it only takes a few hours.

HOW THE COURT WORKS

- When the Judge sees that you are representing yourself, he may well give you an assurance that he will keep you fully informed of what everything means. It is his job to ensure you understand what is happening.

- Ask him a question whenever you like.

- The proceedings may go like this :

  i) **The Judge** will begin by saying what the hearing is for and explain how he wants to deal with matters.

  ii) **Your wife's barrister** will say briefly that she wants a divorce and why.

  iii) **You** will say briefly why she should not get a divorce, and anything else important that you need to explain at the beginning.

  iv) **Your wife goes into the Witness Box.**

    Her barrister will ask her questions, and she will answer, stating her reasons for wanting to divorce you and what evidence she says she has.

    You will question her about her motives and her evidence.

45

(Have all your questions written down well before the hearing.)

v) **You go into the Witness Box.**

You will give your evidence that the marriage has <u>not</u> broken down irretrievably and that your wife's grounds for divorce are false.

Your wife's barrister questions you about your marriage, your reasons for contesting the divorce, and anything else he thinks is relevant.

vi) **Your wife's witnesses (if she has any) go into the Witness Box.**

Your wife's barrister will question them on what they know about your marriage (and about any written statement they may have made).

You will question them (if you want to) to show that what they say is not true or not relevant.

vii) **Your witnesses (if you have any) go into the Witness Box.**

You will question them to get them to give whatever useful information they have (and about any written statement they have made).

Your wife's barrister will question them.

viii) **Your wife's barrister will summarize her reasons for divorce and evidence.**

ix) **You will summarize your reasons for opposing her divorce.**

Including :

evidence that the marriage has not broken down irretrievably,
evidence that the grounds for divorce, in her Petition, are false,
evidence of any perjury by her in court, or in documents,
any ulterior motives she has for divorcing you,
any very bad behaviour by her,
and anything else you think is relevant.

x) **The Judge** may then retire for a time to consider his decision. When he returns, he will say whether he is going to grant a divorce (and issue a decree nisi), or refuse it.

YOUR DEFENCE

- **You should show, at all times, that you are a reasonable man and have always treated your wife reasonably.**

- **Your defence should be of two kinds :**

  i) Expose Lies and Falsehoods

  Expose lies and falsehoods in her divorce Petition and other documents.

  ii) Disprove her Grounds for Divorce

  You will show that the marriage has not broken down irretrievably and her grounds for divorce, given in her Petition, are not true.

- See below.

EXPOSE LIES AND FALSEHOODS

- **Deliberate lies, exaggerations and falsehoods are common in divorce Petitions. But, they are unacceptable and illegal.**

- Look at your wife's divorce Petition very carefully. Identify everything that is untrue. If she put in any lie, <u>knowing that it was untrue</u>, that is **"perjury"**.

- Perjury is a serious criminal offence. Perjury to defraud you of assets is a very serious criminal offence, with grave consequences for her. You can ask that the matter is referred to the criminal courts for her prosecution.

- Look at all the other documents that she has produced for courts to support her divorce. If there are deliberate falsehoods, that is also perjury.

- Well before the court hearing, make a list of all false statements by her that you have found. Get all the written evidence you can of each falsehood. Send a copy to the Judge several days before the hearing. Take several copies with you to the hearing.

- Not only does perjury lead to prosecution, it also crucially undermines her case for a divorce from you and the seizure of your assets. If she has done this, she should get nothing from you.

- **It is fundamental to Justice that no-one should benefit from committing a crime.** If the Judge does give her a divorce, even though she has committed perjury, you should make full use of her perjury at the later financial hearing, and say that she should get nothing.

- If you can prove perjury in a contested divorce hearing, you have a good chance of preventing both a divorce and the seizure of your assets. You can tell the Judge that it is unlawful for him to give her either. You can take the matter to the European Courts if he does.

DISPROVE HER GROUNDS FOR DIVORCE

- **To get a divorce, your wife must prove that your marriage has "broken down irretrievably". That it is impossible to mend it.**

  Your defence must be that the marriage has not broken down irretrievably.

  Despite difficulties, it can and should be repaired.

  If you have children, they are a major factor for preserving the marriage. There is a great weight of evidence to show that children, and teenagers, are seriously damaged by divorce. (See "Shameful and Despised".)

  Your defence can also include:

  i) the things that you and your wife have done together, particularly in the last year,

  ii) the support you give her, including accommodation, money, emotional support and help with the children,

  iii) anything else that shows that you can soon return to normal domestic life,

  Emphasise any ulterior motives that your wife has to abandon you, such as "enrichment" from seizing your possessions.

- **To get a divorce, she must <u>also</u> show clear evidence of one, or more, of the following five facts :**

i) Adultery <u>and</u> she finds it intolerable to live with you.

Adultery is heterosexual intercourse between a married person and a member of the opposite sex, who is not their spouse. And, sexual penetration must occur.

Homosexual, or lesbian, sex does not count as adultery.

(The person with whom your wife says you had sex is called the "co-respondent". She does not have to be named. But if she is named, she has the right to take part in the court hearing, if she wants to.)

Your defence can include:

<u>*Your marriage is not irretrievably broken and can be saved and repaired.*</u>
If you can deny penetrative sex with another woman, this is the basis of your defence.

You should also produce as much evidence as you can that your wife has shown signs of forgiving you for any love affair you have had, so it is obvious that it is not intolerable for her to live with you.

It is difficult to prove penetrative sex has occurred without an admission from one of those who did it. It may have just been a close cuddle.

Your wife cannot use adultery by you, as grounds for divorce, if she has continued to live with you <u>as man and wife for 6 months</u>, from the date she says she discovered your adultery. After that the Judge will say she has forgiven you.

Perhaps your wife's motives for divorce are just cynical monetary gain.

ii) Unreasonable Behaviour

This is the most popular ground for seeking divorce, because it is vague and woolly. It is a matter of opinion what "unreasonable" means.

Your wife is supposed to demonstrate that you have behaved so badly that she cannot reasonably be expected to live with you. She must prove that your behaviour has been terrible and gone well beyond the irritations and silliness that we all live with every day.

She may claim that you are miserly, neglectful, threatening, violent, a drunkard and sexually over demanding. Be ready to refute everything in her Petition that is untrue.

Your defence can include:

The marriage has not broken down irretrievably, and can be repaired.
Give reasons that it would be wrong to dissolve the marriage.

You should insist that she produce evidence that is objective, tangible and conclusive of what she claims is your "unreasonable behaviour".

It is a strong factor in your favour if you can give evidence of irrational, provocative and unacceptable behaviour by her, that you have dealt with calmly and with restraint. This shows that you are sensible and level-headed, while her evidence is flawed and unreliable.

You can say that your behaviour is not much different from other people's, and life in your home has been normal and ordinary. It is entirely fitting that she should continue to live with you, as your wife, if she wants to enjoy your property.

Emphasis that she has ulterior motives to steal your property or separate you from your children.

iii) Desertion

This means that your wife claims that you have deserted her for a continuous period of 2 years. It also means that she has not had any of the normal benefits of marriage from you, and you deserted her against her will.

She must prove that :

a) You have both been living totally separate lives for a continuous period of 2 years, before she issued her Petition.
   (Short periods when you came together to patch up differences are disregarded, but are not counted as part of the 2 years.)

b) When you left her, you had decided that the marriage was finished and the separation was permanent.

Your defence can include:

Your marriage is not irretrievably broken and you can successfully keep it going.

You can disprove desertion by showing that :

a) She consented to a separation.

b) You had a reasonable cause to leave her temporarily.
For example: because of your work or studies, or illness, or family commitments.

c) You left because of her unreasonable behaviour, and she was to blame.

d) She consented to the separation, or you started living together again.

iv) Separation for Two Years with Consent

This means that you have not lived together as a married couple for a continuous period of at least 2 years, and for most of that time you have lived in separate accommodation. This is different from desertion because she must also show that you now consent to the divorce.

The 2 years must be immediately before she makes her Petition. Short periods when you lived together are disregarded, but do not count towards the 2 years.

She must show that you have given your consent freely, that there was no unreasonable pressure on you to agree and you fully understand the effect divorce will have on your life.

You defence can include:

Your marriage has not broken down irretrievably.

You can disprove her claim that you have been separated for 2 years, and you can say that you have not given your consent freely and with full understanding of what it meant.

v) Five Years Separation

She must prove that you have lived apart for 5 years, or longer, immediately before she made her Petition. If this is true, she does not need your consent for a divorce.

A period when you lived together during this time, not longer than 6 months, is disregarded.

Your defence can include:

<u>*Your marriage has not broken down irretrievably.*</u>
Give all the evidence that you can.

If possible, show evidence that you have in fact lived together for longer than 6 months during the last 5 years. If you can prove this, then she must start counting the 5 year period from the time you last parted.

OPEN COURT

- It is the law that a contested divorce hearing must be held in open court, to which the Public has access. This is a good thing because you are more likely to get justice when a Judge knows that he is being scrutinized by others.

- If the Judge tries to hold the hearing in closed court, you can say that the Family Proceedings Rules 1991, Rule 2.28(1) require an open court. The proceedings will be void if he does not comply. If you decided to appeal, the Appeal Court would be bound to allow an appeal on that ground alone.

BE PREPARED BEFORE THE HEARING

- Well before the hearing, make notes of everything that you want to say. If you think it will be easier, write out word for word what you want to say, then you can just read it.

- Make a list of all the questions that you want to ask your wife. If there will be witnesses, make a list of the questions you will ask each.

- Check with your solicitor, well before the hearing, that you have not left anything out.

A WRITTEN RECORD

- You should make notes of all important facts at the hearing.

- When the Judge gives his decision, at the end of the hearing, write down as much as you can about the decision and his reasons. This will be your only detailed record of what has happened.

- If you intend to appeal, or go to the European Courts, you should use your rough notes to write a detailed statement of the hearing. Do this as soon as possible after the hearing.

- See Annex 8.

COSTS

- If you contest your wife's divorce, but the Judge decides she should get it, he may also decide that you should be forced to pay the costs of her lawyers.

- Well before the hearing, consult your solicitor about all the costs you may incur.

- See "What Happens Next - Step 12" .

- See Annex 8 - "A Divorce Suit Record" .

- See "Appeals" .

- See "The European Courts" .

CHILDREN

YOUR FIRST DECISION

- If you have children, you should think carefully about what you want for them if you and your wife divorce or separate.

- **It is your fundamental right that your children live with you after you are divorced or separated.**

- **Many men decide that they want their children to live with them for most of the time after divorce or separation.**

- **If you want this, you will have to confront the unjust courts and biased "Welfare Officers".**

- <u>**But you can win. Many others have.**</u>

VITAL THINGS TO KEEP IN MIND

- **If you want custody of your children after court proceedings, it is vital that you stay with them during the proceedings. Stay with them at all costs.**

- **If custody is what you want, it is important that you <u>say repeatedly</u> why <u>it is in the best interests of your children that they live with you</u>. This is the argument that will get you custody.**

- **Keep saying that you have the strongest parent-child relationship with them and are the best person to care for them. Disruption to their lives must be minimized by keeping you and them together.**

- **It is a powerful advantage if your children say repeatedly that they want to live with you. But if they do not say this, it may be because they lack the maturity to know what is best for them.**

SPEAK TO YOUR CHILDREN

- Speak to your children when your wife is not there. You may want to explain why she is breaking up your family. Say that you will try to stop this but, if she succeeds, they can live with you for most of the time if they want to. Reassure them they will be secure and loved with you.

- **If your children say that they would prefer to live with you, make a written note of what they say and when. Do everything in your power to support them in this. If they are old enough, you can suggest that they write their own letter to the judge saying what they want.**

- Alternatively, if you prefer that your children will live with your wife, you will want the court to tell her bluntly that you will have access whenever you want it. Say that you will expect financial compensation and other penalties if she does not comply.

- **Remember, that if your wife takes your children from you, she will use this as an excuse to seize most, or all, of your property. She will also demand a large part of your future income as maintenance for the children and probably for herself.**

- See the Steps that deal with children in "What Happens Next".

CHILDREN TREATED BADLY

- **Judges, "Welfare Officers" and others who run the divorce system pay cynical lip service to the welfare of children. They pretend that children are one of their main concerns and you will hear a lot of humbug from them about this.**

- What really happens is that these people use children to make divorce easier and more lucrative for women who are deserting their husband.

- "Welfare Officers" (or CAFCASS Officers) are social workers who work for the divorce courts. One will interview you, your wife and any children who are old enough to understand what is happening to them.

- The "Welfare Officer" will then write a report for the judge. This will recommend which parent your children should live with after divorce. She may also appear at court to defend what she has written.

- "Welfare Officers" have a bad reputation. They are feminist and heavily biased in favour of persuading children to say that they want to live with their mother. They are experienced at putting pressure on children when they interview them, at asking leading questions and putting words into children's mouths.

THE WELFARE OFFICER'S REPORT

- **You will be sent a copy of the "Welfare Officer's" written report about your children. If it is biased, you should write to the court office immediately. Say that the report is biased, that it contains false information and you want the judge to disregard it.**

- **Repeat your complaint when you get to court. Tell the judge that there will be serious trouble if the false report is not rejected.**

- **You can say that you are considering action against the "Welfare Officer" in the European Court of Human Rights.**

- See "European Courts".

WHY DO THEY DO IT ?

- The main purpose of marriage is to provide children with a secure and stable home, with both parents, until they are old enough to fend for themselves. The unjust divorce courts have no interest in this.

- What these courts do is to make divorce as easy as possible for women deserting their husbands, even when this is unlawful. The courts do this by seizing the property, pensions and income of men.

- They like to give women custody of children and then use the children to justify seizing men's assets. These are the reasons that women apply for 70% of all divorces.

ACT QUICKLY IF SHE TAKES YOUR CHILDREN

- **If your wife takes your children away from your home without a judge's agreement, it is important that you go to court as fast as you can to get them back.**

- **Ask your solicitor how to get an emergency hearing for a court order to have your children returned.**

- Tell the court that your wife is acting irresponsibly for selfish reasons. She is disregarding their welfare and is not to be trusted to care for children by herself. Say that the children's best interests are in living with you and ask the judge to tell your wife not to abduct them again.

- The longer that your wife is able to keep your children away from you, the more difficult it will be for you to get them back. Your wife will say that they have got used to living with her and it would be too upsetting for them to return to you.

- **If you want custody of your children, you must stay with them during divorce proceedings, at all costs.**

YOUR CHILDREN SHOULD LIVE WITH YOU

If you want your children to live with you for most of the time after divorce or separation, it is important that you :

- **Write a "Child Residence Statement" for the court.**
  Your Statement will say why it is best for your children to live with you and not your wife. Give the judge lots of reasons why your children should live with you.

- **When you write it, concentrate on the reasons that it is essential for your children's welfare that they live with you. Say in detail how you will look after them from day to day. See below.**

- **Include any reasons that your wife is not suitable to have your children live with her permanently. See below.**

- **But, do say that you will do everything you can to encourage close and frequent contact between the children and your wife.**

- Type your Statement if you can, or write it neatly by hand. Ask your solicitor when you should send the Statement to the court manager. Keep a copy for yourself, your solicitor and your wife's solicitor.

- Consider what witnesses you can bring to court to say that your children should live with you in future. These can include relatives, friends neighbours, your GP or another reliable specialist.

- See the example of a "Child Residence Statement" in Annex 6.

THIS IS WHAT IS BEST FOR YOUR CHILDREN

Your main argument will be that <u>it is best for your children's welfare that they live with you</u> for most of the time in future.

Consider these reasons :

- **You are their most stable and supportive parent.**
  Even in difficult times, you have tried to keep together the family and home where they feel secure. You did this for their benefit not yours.

- **Your children come to you with their problems for comfort and advice.**
  You give them constant love and emotional support.

- **You protect your children when your wife has a temper or emotional outburst.**
  They would be vulnerable if they lived with her and you were not there.

- **Your children prefer to live with you.**
  If they are given a free choice without pressure from your wife, "Welfare Officers" and the school psychologist, they will want to live with you.

- **You are the main homemaker and provider for your children.**
  You have provided them with a home and most of their other needs. If you are separated from them, your resources will be spread too thinly between two homes. Only you can give them what they need in your own home.

- **You are their main help with homework, doing school work on the Internet and planning their education.**

HOW YOU WILL LOOK AFTER THEM

You should say in your Statement exactly how you will care for your children when they reside with you.

Decide these matters :

- **Where you will live with your children and how you will pay for it.**
  Is it essential that all your children live together?
  (Judges are often reluctant to separate siblings.)

- **Where they will go to school.**
  How they will get to school and return home. Who will give them breakfast and their evening meal.

- **Who will care for them during school holidays.**
  Make convincing arrangements with anyone who is going to help. Get them to confirm this in a letter.

- **Whether you will continue to work.**
  If your children are small, you may have to give up full time work. Find out what State benefits you are entitled to. Get the literature and speak to the social security people about this. You can return to work as soon as it suits you after the divorce or separation.

- **What support your relatives (and other helpers) can give with your children in the future.**
  If you work, this is particularly important during school holidays. Ask anyone who is going to help to write a letter confirming what he or she will do. If you are sure they are reliable, attach a copy of the letter to your Statement.

Get everything confirmed in writing to show the judge.

The greater the effort you make, the greater your chance of success.

THINGS YOU SHOULD DO

You must show that you are at the centre of your children's lives.

You probably do all these things already :

- **Take a full interest in your children and everything they do.**
  Make sure that you know all about their activities at school and at home. Involve yourself in their interests and problems.

- **Give them extra love and emotional support.**
  Talk to your children about their mother's divorce, her lack of concern for your family and the future.

- **Play a full part in caring for them.**
  Cook at least some of their food and go shopping for items they need. Frequently take them for walks and other outings.

- **Speak to your children's teachers.**
  Know what subjects they study and their progress. Ask what you can do at home to help with their school work.

- **Take them to the Doctor and Dentist.**
  Play your part when your children need medical care.

- **Take your children on holiday.**
  Be generous in spending on all things.

- **Demonstrate that you are best suited to give your children love, affection, guidance, a secure home and stable education.**

If you do this, you can show in your Statement that you love your children and can provide for their day-to-day needs. Your wife cannot then claim that only she cares and provides for them.

EVIDENCE IS IMPORTANT

- **Keep a secret diary of everything that you do with, and for, your children. You can then present this to the judge, who decides custody, as evidence of your vital role in your children's lives.**

- Even if the diary only covers a month or two, it greatly strengthens your case. Also keep photographs and any other evidence of your continual involvement with your children. If you and your children are "a team", say so.

- **Get as many responsible people as possible to write letters supporting what you want. Judges like written evidence.**

- Bring some witnesses to a child residence hearing to say your children should live with you. This could include relatives, friends, neighbours, your GP and anyone else who supports you and knows your children well.

- Try to find at least one "expert" who will confirm that your children will suffer permanent emotional damage if they are taken away from you. Judges like anyone who sounds like an "expert". But beware that the "expert" does not turn against you.

- **Your goal is to produce overwhelming proof that your children's best interest is to live with you. Give the judge lots of reasons, and evidence, for leaving your children with you.**

NO MORE BIAS AGAINST FATHERS

- You can say that the suggestion that children need their mother more than their father is sexist, old fashioned, out of date and a relic of the past. You reject it completely, whatever your children's age.

- The "different traditional roles and functions of men and women" in child care are bigoted nonsense. The reality is that you are a better parent than your wife and this is what is important. You are the "primary carer" in most essential respects.

- Your wife's selfish determination to destroy the family that your children depend on is evidence that she is a poor parent. Say that your case is different from others where children have been taken from their father. Give any special reasons you can think of.

YOUR WIFE IS NOT SUITABLE

In your Statement, give all the reasons that your wife should not have your children to live with her in future.

Do not exaggerate trivial faults but consider these reasons :

- **Irresponsibility**

  She is destroying the family that gives your children security and stability. She is putting her own wishes before their welfare.

- **Poor Care in the Past**

  She has failed to care for your children properly in the past and you can give examples.

- **Mental Illness or Unstable Behaviour**

  If she has ever been treated for mental illness, or shown the symptoms, she cannot be suitable to care for children alone. Describe what has happened (and give any medical evidence).

- **Violence**

  If your wife has ever been violent in any way towards you, or your children, she cannot be trusted to care for them alone. You fear for your children's safety. Describe what happened and when. (Women start much domestic violence.)

- **Her Career Comes First**

  If she is a career woman, who puts her work before her family, the children will be better cared for by you.

- **Drink or Drugs**

  If your wife has a history of either, give full details.

- **Abduction**

  If she has already taken your children away from you, without their consent or yours, this shows reckless selfishness. (You should speak to your solicitor and immediately apply for a court order to get them back.)

- **Dishonesty**
  If she has made false accusations against you, or not told the truth about anything else, she is not reliable or trustworthy. Produce evidence.

BE PREPARED FOR HER RESPONSE

- Think of the reasons that your wife will give that your children should live with her. Prepare your answer to what she will say.

- In particular, be prepared for the allegation that you have been violent, even if this is false. It is easy to accuse anyone of this, but difficult for him to disprove. This can seriously damage your chance of getting custody. Be ready to refute it.

- You can send the court written comments about your wife's proposals for where your children should live, or you can just say what you think when you get to court.

- Think of any reasons that she will give that you are not suitable to have your children reside with you. Prepare your answer.

BEWARE OF WELFARE OFFICERS

- Tell any "Welfare Officer" (CAFCASS Officer) who interviews your family that you expect her to be completely impartial and you want your children treated properly. No pressure is to be put on them and no words are to be put into their mouths.

- You should speak to your children before they meet a "Welfare Officer". Tell them that if they want to live with you in future, they must say so as often as possible. It is not enough just to say it once.

- If you have the opportunity to conceal a tape recorder in the room where the "Welfare Officer" will speak to your children, you should do so. This could be invaluable evidence of dishonest practice.

- Your children may have said clearly that they want to live with you in future, but a "Welfare Officer" says that they prefer their mother. The WO will say that they speak frankly to her but not to you. Be ready to refute this. Your children can write letters to the judge.

- You should also speak to your children after they have met a "Welfare Officer". Ask them exactly what was said to them and make a written note of what they remember.

- If pressure of any kind was put on them, if they were asked leading questions, or words were put into their mouths, immediately complain in writing to the court manager. Say that you want the "Welfare Officer's" report disregarded and you are considering action against her in the European Courts.

- You can also write to your Member of Parliament and the Secretary of State at the Department for Constitutional Affairs.

IF YOUR CHILDREN LIVE WITH HER

- If your children are to live with your wife after divorce, you should ask for **"joint custody"** and **"normal living contact"** so that you can see them every day, without restriction. This is what is best for your children, and your wife's preferences are secondary.

- There should be no restriction on regular overnight stays. Your children should stay with you every weekend. Half of all school holidays should be with you and they should spend alternate Christmases with you and your family. If that is what you want.

- Alternatively, you can ask for 50/50 access, with your children spending half of every month with you and half with your wife. This is normal in some other countries.

- If this is what you want, write down in detail how it will work and try to get your wife's agreement before you go to court. Send the judge a copy a week before the child residence hearing.

FINANCE

YOUR MONEY & YOUR WIFE

- **"Ancillary Relief" is the nonsense, legal name for a divorce court seizing your property, pension and other assets for your wife.**

- Theft of men's property is the main incentive for divorce. This is why 70% of divorces are sought by women.

- **The "family courts" like to treat all assets that have been earned, or owned, during a marriage as "marital assets" that can be seized and given to your wife.**

- Property owned by either you, or your wife, before the marriage is supposed to remain with its original owner. However, your home, or other asset that your wife claims you have shared with her, is also liable to be seized.

- **A court will not seize your assets before a "decree nisi" is issued. This piece of paper says that the marriage will end.**

- <u>**It is very important to delay a decree nisi being issued by sending the court an Answer to your wife's divorce Petition.**</u>

- **You can then contest the divorce in court, or negotiate a reasonable settlement.**

- See "Contest the Divorce".

- See the Steps on finance in "What Happens Next".

FINANCIAL DECLARATION

- After you receive your wife's Petition, you will get a demand from the court that you make a financial statement of all your assets and income. This is done on "Form E" that you get from the court office.

- Form E is 20 pages long and demands details of property, furniture, cars, pensions, money, shares, premium bonds, PEPs, TESSAs, ISAs, current income, business interests, trusts and anything else that you have.

Details of all accounts and bank statements for the last 12 months are demanded.

- Your wife's solicitor may ask for further evidence of what you have. Your wife will also complete a Form E and you will get a copy. You should look carefully to see if she has left out anything.

- If you cannot agree a financial settlement with your wife, these forms (and the evidence that you attach) are used by a judge at a court hearing to seize your possessions for your wife.

ACT QUICKLY

- **Before any court hearing about finance, you should spend any cash or other modest assets like shares.**
  If you do not, all or most may be seized for your wife.

- Spend money on things that have no value to your wife, for example :

  i) Clothes for yourself (or children).

  ii) A car for yourself, if she already has one.

  iii) A computer (and other things that devalue quickly).

  iv) Holidays (and treats for your children).

  v) Pay your solicitor in advance.

  A judge is unlikely to criticize you for any expenditure that was on your home (or second home if you have one), your children, or of benefit to your family in any other way.

- It is usually difficult for a judge to get assets back once disposed of. But he will get them back if you simply transfer them into someone else's name, or sell them to a relative at a low price. Also, beware that he might seize other assets for your wife, in place of anything you have disposed of.

- Some men draw their money out of the bank and sell shares and other assets. They pretend to spend it but hide the bank notes, or other valuables, where they cannot be found. Judges do not like this and will penalize you if your wife's solicitor can prove that you have done it.

- The men who do this consult their solicitors in advance about what checks and investigations their wife's solicitor will make about hidden assets.

- Other men, who keep their assets in safe countries abroad, go there to live and avoid the courts. Anything left behind is stolen.

- See "Forward Planning".

USE YOUR OWN JUDGEMENT

- Well before any court hearing about finance, ask your solicitor what he thinks the court will give to your wife. Be cautious about accepting his advice. Solicitors advising men will sometimes give away too much. But his opinion is based on what he has seen these courts do to men, so keep it in mind.

- Remember, that if the judge at a court hearing about finance thinks that you have offered your wife too little, he will try to increase what she gets and try to make you pay her costs.

- See "Avoiding Her Costs".

DISHONEST AND IMPRACTICAL IDEAS

- The main function of the divorce courts is to seize the assets of honest men for wives who are deserting them. Theft by divorce is then used to finance the abduction of men's children.

- **Judges base their seizure of men's assets on confused and misguided ideas. This is what they think :**

  i) **Your wife should be in the same financial position after the divorce that she was before it.**

  You can say that this is absurd and impractical. There is not enough money to go round. She is an able-bodied adult. She will have to provide for herself when she is no longer your wife.

  ii) **Your assets should be divided according to the "needs" of the two parties. She should get as much of your property and income as she needs for herself and any children.**

This is theft. No civilized society now allocates assets on a Marxist basis.

iii) "The yardstick of equality" means that your wife should get most of your property and other assets.

You can say that the only sensible "yardstick of equality" takes into account the financial input of both parties into the marriage. You contributed most and it is your right to keep it. Anything else treats women like children.

iv) The "homemaker" (your wife) should not be discriminated against.

You can say that you are also a "homemaker". You have also made the largest financial contribution to the marriage and you expect to keep most of what is yours. Anything else is theft and discriminates against you.

v) Your assets should be divided on a "no fault basis".

You can say "no fault means no justice" and you do not want that. (Be careful if your behaviour has also been bad.)

vi) Bad behaviour by your wife should be ignored when giving her your assets.

Judges like to ignore bad behaviour by your wife. But they must to take it into account if has been both "obvious and gross".

You can say : "Her behaviour has been both obvious and gross. I insist that it is taken into account and her share of my property substantially reduced. I will appeal if you do not".

If you want to use this, write down the details of her behaviour and send it to the court before the hearing on finance.

vii) It is irrelevant that your wife has committed perjury to get her divorce and she is unscrupulous in breaking her marriage contract.

It is the law that she should get nothing if this is true. No-one should benefit from committing a criminal offence or breaking a contract.

If you say this, a judge may tell you that you should have a contested divorce hearing. If you do not want one, you can say that you have no confidence in getting a just verdict. The costs would be too high and you cannot afford justice under the English legal system.

- The law for seizing your possessions is the Matrimonial Causes Act 1973 Section 25 (1) & (2). (See "Matrimonial Causes Act 1973".)

A REASONABLE SETTLEMENT

- Your wife should not get any reward for breaking her marriage contract and abandoning you. If there was anything untrue in her Petition, then her divorce is based on perjury. Giving her any of your assets for this is corrupt, unjust and unlawful.

- You want assets distributed in the same proportion that each party contributed to the marriage. If she is deserting you, this is the only fair solution. If her contribution to the marriage was in "money's worth", then perhaps she should take "money's worth" as her share of the assets. This is the only proper "yardstick of equality".

- You do not expect your wife to reimburse you for the financial benefits that you have given her during marriage. The other side of this coin is that she should not steal from you now if the marriage is to end.

- Like your wife, you are a "homemaker". You have also paid for most of what you both have and this must be taken into account when dividing assets.

- See "Negotiation".

FIGHT TO THE END

- If your solicitor says that you can expect to lose all, or almost all, your property (and children), you may want to fight on through many appeals. Ask your solicitor whether there is any litigation against your wife that you could start under laws other than the Matrimonial Causes Act.

- You can build up large costs of your own by employing barristers in court. Then there will be nothing left for your wife either. (You may even win in the end.)

- If the English courts try to prevent you from repeatedly appealing, you can go to the European Courts. (See "European Courts".)

- You may be left with nothing and have to start again. But you will have the satisfaction of not giving in to thievery and injustice. You will be able to look your children in the eye in years to come and say that you did what you could to fight for their interests.

MAKE A WILL

- You should make a new will as soon as you know that you may be in the divorce courts. You can write it yourself, in your own hand-writing and witnessed by a friend, or get a solicitor to do it. Keep the will (and any photocopies) in a safe place, such as your bank or with relatives.

- If you die before a decree absolute is issued, your wife will expect to seize assets, whatever your wishes.

- If you die after a decree absolute, leaving a will made before a divorce, any provision for your former wife is supposed to become ineffective (unless you have stated otherwise).

- But, even if you do make a new will, beware that she may still go to court when you die, and demand still more of your possessions. This is a particular danger if she does not remarry. You live in a country in which nothing is safe.

- Consult your solicitor.

TAXATION

- If you have large assets, divorce may have tax consequences for you.

- In particular, there may be a liability for capital gains tax, if you are forced to give away property (but not money).

- Consult your accountant, or other adviser, as soon you can.

- See "Forward Planning" .

- See "A Secure Future" .

APPEALS

YOUR RIGHT TO APPEAL

- **You can appeal against :**

    i)   The granting of a divorce

    ii) A child residence order

    iii) A financial order

    iv) Any other order made against you.

- **You must fill in a form called a "Notice of Appeal". Send it to the office of the court you are appealing to.**

- **You must do this within a time limit. (This is usually 7 or 14 days from the date on the order you are appealing against).**

- If you miss the time limit, you can send an **"out of time" appeal**. But this is a last resort. Say in a letter to the court manager that you are representing yourself and, if your appeal is not considered, you will appeal to the European Courts.

- The court office will write back to you giving a date for the appeal hearing. This will probably be months in the future.

- **If there was a mistake or misrepresentation at the previous hearing, you can tell the court office that you want that hearing held again. But do not miss the deadline for an appeal while you are waiting for a decision.**

TO APPEAL OR NOT APPEAL ?

- **There are 2 different reasons for making an appeal :**

    i) <u>Either</u> **to make a genuine appeal.**

        This is with the intention of going to the appeal court and having an unjust order overruled.

ii) **Or**   **to make a "tactical" appeal.**

> This is with the intention of offering to withdraw it if your wife agrees to pay her own lawyers' bill or agrees to something else you want.

- Appeals cause long delay and your wife will be keen to avoid them. But if you make a tactical appeal and she refuses to compromise, you will have to decide whether to go to the appeal court or withdraw your appeal anyway.

- Think carefully about what you are appealing against and what it is you want instead. Consult your solicitor about your grounds for appealing, your chance of success and the cost.

- Remember that if you go to the appeal court and loose, your wife will ask that you are forced to pay her lawyers' bill for the hearing. (This may be £2,000 or more.) Also, if you go to the appeal court, she may appeal herself and change her own demands.

- Represent yourself at an appeal hearing. Only get a barrister to speak for you if you are deliberately using up your assets so that there is nothing left for your wife to seize.

GROUNDS FOR APPEAL

- **Injustice is always ground for appeal.**

   Also, consider the following grounds :

   i) A judge made a decision against the great weight of evidence.

   ii) A judge "abused his powers of discretion" or "misdirected himself".

   iii) A judge got a question of law wrong.
   For example, under the Matrimonial Causes Act 1973.

   iv) A judge abused your rights (or your children's rights) under the Common Law, the European Convention on Human Rights or the Human Rights Act 1998.

   v) New evidence has come to light that the judge did not know about.

- **Consult your solicitor.**

TO WHICH COURT SHOULD YOU APPEAL?

- Appeals can be made to: the High Court, the Appeal Court or The House of Lords. (You can also take action in the European Courts). The right court for your appeal will depend on what you are appealing against.

- Ask your solicitor to tell you the right appeal court. He will also know what procedures you should follow.

- You are entitled to **"direct assistance"** from the staff in the court office of any appeal court. It is their job to advise you on filling out appeal forms, deadlines, fees and court procedures. You can visit them, write to them, or telephone, as often as you like.

- There is a very large fee for taking an appeal to the House of Lords. Their Lordships don't work cheap.

HOW TO APPEAL

- **If you decide to appeal against any order, you should write your own statement of the judge's decision that you are appealing against (include the reasons he gave).**

- Use the notes that you made in court to type the statement (or write it neatly by hand).

- Your wife's solicitor, or her clerk, may produce a written statement of any court hearing. Ask for a copy for yourself and your solicitor. If it is accurate, or if you can agree amendments with her solicitor, it may save you the trouble of writing your own.

- You will need the statement when you get to the appeal hearing to explain what it is you are appealing against.

- **Get a "Notice of Appeal" form.** Your solicitor may have one or you can telephone the court office of the court you are appealing to. Ask what fee has to be paid for the appeal.

- Get your appeal to the appeal court's office before the deadline.

  Include the following :

  i) The completed **Notice of Appeal form (and one photocopy)**

  ii) **The fee**

  iii) **A copy of your statement (This is optional).**

- For an example of a "Notice of Appeal" form see Annex 12.

- See "The European Courts" .

- See "Avoiding Her Costs" .

LEGAL AID

WHAT IS IT ?

- **Legal Aid is money provided by the Legal Services Commission (LSC) to pay the bills of lawyers' working for you in England (or Wales).** (The LSC used to be called the Legal Aid Board.)

- You only get Legal Aid if you are "eligible". If you get Legal Aid, you may still have to pay a part of your solicitor's bill from your income or savings (or borrow).

- **If you have any property or money left after divorce proceedings, you will have to pay back all, or some, of the Legal Aid.**

- **The LSC may take a "charge" on your home.** This means that you do not have to repay the Legal Aid loan until the property is sold, which may be far in the future. (You can repay it sooner, if you want to.)

ARE YOU ELIGIBLE ?

- **You may be eligible for Legal Aid if your :**

    i) **Gross income (before tax etc) is less than £2,288 per month** before deducting tax and bills (if you live with a partner, other than your wife, her income is included), and

    ii) **Disposable income is less than £632 per month** after deducting tax, mortgage costs or rent, maintenance, child care costs (if you have paid work) and about £150 for each dependant, and

    iii) **Disposable Capital is less than £8,000** including property (see below), money (or money owed to you), investments, insurance policies, business assets and other valuables (but not your car and home contents, unless they are of exceptional value).

    Disposable Capital includes:

    The value of your home in excess of £100,000, after deducting any mortgage (up to a maximum of £100,000), **plus**

Any equity in other property.

(The maximum deducted for all mortgages, on all property, is £100,000.)

- The LSC considers your case under their "Funding Code", before they give Legal Aid. If they think your case is weak, you will not get it.

FINDING OUT ABOUT IT

- You can get a leaflet on Legal Aid, from the LSC, called "A Practical Guide to Community Legal Service funding" (tel: 0845 3000 343, or the LSC website).

  LSC Customer Services (tel: 020 7759 0000) will answer your questions.

  The LSC's website is: **www.legalservices.gov.uk**

  Other information is on: **www.justask.org.uk**

SHOULD YOU APPLY ?

- <u>**You should always apply for Legal Aid if you think you are eligible.**</u>

- **But you should still represent yourself in the divorce to keep down costs. In this way Legal Aid acts as a useful, interest-free loan.**

- **If you have Legal Aid, this prevents your wife from forcing you to pay her lawyers' bill if she wins in any court hearing.**

BE CAUTIOUS WITH LEGAL AID

- **For most men, Legal Aid can be a financial trap.** It encourages you to spend a lot of money on lawyers' bills that you will have to pay back after the divorce.

- **Represent yourself, with a solicitor's support.**

- Most wives divorcing their husbands get unlimited Legal Aid, but many men do not qualify for it because of their higher income.

HOW IT WORKS

- **You should complete the Legal Aid application form yourself.** Get the form from your solicitor.

- Your solicitor will send your completed form to the LSC. Keep a photocopy for yourself.

- If you are successful, you will be sent a LSC Funding Certificate saying what you can spend Legal Aid on. The money will be sent direct to your solicitor.

- **Ask your solicitor what benefits you will get from your Legal Aid and <u>how much you will have to pay back.</u>**

BECOMING UNEMPLOYED

- **You are more likely to qualify for Legal Aid if you are unemployed.**

  No court can make you work.

- Your income will be low, and you are more likely to get Legal Aid, if you:

  i) are made redundant, or

  ii) cannot work because of stress and the divorce, or

  iii) have stopped work to spend more time with your children.

  Most people take a career break at some time in their lives.

- You must think carefully about how you will pay for accommodation, food etc if you do this. Find out what State benefits you (and your children) will get. See your doctor about any symptoms you have got, and get a letter from him as evidence.

- Becoming unemployed may also help if you want your children to reside with you permanently. It gives you a lot of free time to look after them, which is a strong argument you can put to the court.

- You can return to work when it suits you.

- See "Children".

DISGRACEFUL DISCRIMINATION

- The Legal Aid system is biased and discriminates against men :

    i)   A man who works is usually refused Legal Aid to defend himself against his Legally Aided wife.

    ii)   A man is prevented from claiming costs against his Legally Aided wife when he successfully defends himself at a court hearing.

    iii)   A wife's solicitor doubles her Legally Aided costs when the husband is forced to pay them.

- This means that a Legally Aided wife has a bottomless purse to pay lawyers, but her husband is often impoverished.

- If you win at a court hearing, you may be able to claim your costs back against the LSC if they gave your wife Legal Aid. You would have to show that you have suffered grave financial hardship, and they make this as difficult as possible. Consult your solicitor.

- See "Costs" .

CONTEST YOUR WIFE'S LEGAL AID

- If your wife is given Legal Aid, her solicitor will send you a copy of her Legal Aid certificate.

- If you think that she has understated her income or capital to obtain Legal Aid, you can object to her getting it.

- Write to the LSC at 85 Gray's Inn Road, London WC1X 8TX (tel: 020 7759 0000), or their nearest office on the back page of their leaflet.

- Say what her income and capital are. (Enclose evidence if you have any.) Ask for her Legal Aid certificate to be withdrawn.

- If she has attempted fraud, that is a criminal offence.

COSTS

YOUR COSTS

- Costs are the money that you have to pay in divorce proceedings. The main cost is lawyers' bills. You may also be forced to pay conveyancing fees (if your property is sold) and other expenses.

- **The total cost of solicitor's support while you represent yourself may be £1,000 to £2,000. This compares with £10,000 to £15,000 for an average divorce if you do not represent yourself and have lawyers do it.**

- **Solicitors often suggest that you have a barrister to speak for you at court hearings. Barristers are like solicitors but more long-winded and much more expensive. You do not need one. Speak to the judge yourself, he is only human.**

- **Ask your solicitor regularly what his support is costing you. Then you will not be surprised by a large unexpected bill.**

YOUR WIFE'S COSTS

- **Your wife's costs may be £10,000 to £30,000 or more for an average divorce.**
  She may have been given Legal Aid to divorce you.

- **Your wife will demand that the court forces you to pay her costs.**
  Even if she has Legal Aid, her costs can still be forced onto you.

- Her costs are so high because the unjust courts allow her solicitor to double her bill when you are forced to pay.

- **You may be forced to pay some or all of your wife's costs if :**

  i) **You do not contest the divorce.**

     If you do not send the court office an Answer to your wife's Petition, then you are accepting the blame for the divorce. You will be forced to pay all her costs as well as your own.

ii) **You withdraw your Answer without her agreeing to pay her own costs.**

If you withdraw your Answer you are accepting the blame for the divorce. You must get her to agree to pay her own costs in return for you withdrawing your Answer. If you do not do this, you will be forced to pay all your own costs and hers.

iii) **You contest the divorce but lose after a divorce suit hearing and she gets her divorce.**

iv) **Any of your wife's demands on finance, children etc are accepted by the court (or you make an appeal and lose).**

You may be forced to pay her costs whenever your wife succeeds in getting something that she wants. If you resist the theft of your property, or try to stop her taking away your children, but lose after a court hearing, you may be forced to pay her costs for that hearing.

IF YOU WIN

- If any court hearing gives a decision in your favour, you can ask that your wife pay your costs for that hearing. You can claim the cost of help from your solicitor. You can also claim for the time that you have spent preparing for that hearing at £9.25 per hour.

- But if she has got Legal Aid, you may be refused.

- See "Legal Aid" - "Disgraceful Discrimination" .

- **See "Avoiding Her Costs" .**

AVOIDING HER COSTS

Here are ways to avoid having to pay your wife's costs. These can save you a lot of money.

AN ANSWER TO HER PETITION

- **Whatever your plans for the future, you must contest her divorce by sending an Answer to your wife's divorce Petition. <u>This is vital.</u>**

- **Think carefully about whether to continue to contest the divorce to a "divorce suit hearing". This is the only certain way to protect your property, pension and children.**

- But, if your wife can prove the allegations in her Petition, you will lose. You will then be forced to pay her costs for that hearing. Remember that these unjust courts are biased against men and favour divorce.

A "TACTICAL" ANSWER

- **When you send an Answer to your wife's Petition, this gives you a negotiating position. If you want to, you can offer to withdraw your Answer if she agrees to pay her own costs (and a reasonable divorce settlement). This is called a "tactical" Answer.**

- Contested divorce court hearings are often a year or longer after the issue of the Petition. If at first your wife is reluctant to pay her own costs, you can afford to wait. Say that you really are determined to contest the divorce in court.

- **Before you withdraw an Answer, you should get your wife's written agreement to pay her own costs for all divorce matters, ancillary relief (seizing your assets), child residence and anything else that she has spent money on.**

- **This is also the time to negotiate a financial settlement.**

- See "Contest the Divorce" .

A "TACTICAL" APPEAL

- You are entitled to appeal against any court order that is made that you do not like. This means getting the right form from the court office, filling it in and paying a fee.

- You can make an appeal and then offer to withdraw it if your wife agrees to pay her own costs. This is called a "tactical" appeal. Do not tell anyone that your appeal is tactical. Always say that it is a genuine appeal.

- Appeals cause long delay and your wife will be keen to avoid them. There is a time limit for making an appeal, often 7 or 14 days after the date of the order you are appealing against. Get your appeal back to the court office in time.

- If you do miss a time limit, send the appeal by post with the correct fee. Include a letter saying that you are representing yourself and, if your appeal is not considered, you will go to the European Courts.

- See "Appeals".

A "TACTICAL" APPLICATION

- You can apply for a court order demanding that your wife does something that you want. Consult your solicitor about what you can demand. Applications cause delay and your wife will be keen to avoid them.

- You can make an application and then withdraw it if your wife agrees to pay some or all of her own costs for her divorce. This is called a "tactical" application. Do not tell anyone that your application is tactical. Always say that it is a genuine application.

- If your wife refuses to pay her own costs, you will then have to decide whether to continue with the application or withdraw it anyway.

A "CALDERBANK LETTER"

- A **"Calderbank" offer** is a letter that you send to your wife before a court hearing about finance. The purpose is to avoid paying her costs for the hearing if the judge agrees that your offer was reasonable and she did not accept it.

- The letter states the maximum that you are prepared to give her. At the top of the letter write **"Without prejudice save as to costs"** .

- The judge will not see the letter until after he has decided how much of your assets she should get. If his judgement agrees with your offer, you can produce your "Calderbank letter" and say that you should not pay any of her costs.

- If she does not have Legal Aid, she may also be liable to pay your costs.

- Consult your solicitor about how to write a "Calderbank letter".

LEGAL AID

- <u>**Always apply for Legal Aid if you think you qualify.**</u>
  It is an interest free loan. But, if you have income or assets, you will have to repay it after the proceedings.

- **If you are on Legal Aid, your wife cannot make you pay her costs.**

- See "Negotiation" .

- See "Legal Aid" .

A CLEAN BREAK

- If there is to be a divorce, you should always ask for a **"clean break"**. This means that your wife cannot claim maintenance for herself from you in the future. Over the years, maintenance can add up to even more than value of assets seized in the divorce.

- If your wife gets maintenance (even "nominal maintenance" of 50p a year) she can demand much more in future. You will never be rid of her.

- If she does get nominal maintenance, wait for a sensible time and then ask her to agree to a **"clean break order"**. You can say that if she refuses she will have to appear in court and may pay your costs.

- If she agrees, consult your solicitor. He will give you a "Consent Minute of Order", financial disclosure forms and anything else that you and she must complete to get a clean break from a court. Do all this by post.

AVOIDING EVICTION

STAY IN YOUR HOME

- **It is your fundamental right to remain in your home unless you wish to leave. Any attempt to evict you, because that is what your wife wants, contravenes your Common Law rights and the European Convention on Human Rights.**

- If you own all or part of your home, you should stay there until all financial matters connected with the divorce are settled. You may wish to stay there permanently after separation or divorce.

- If you leave your home before a settlement, it weakens your hold on the equity that you have paid for. If you have children, leaving weakens your link to them.

STAND FIRM

- Your wife's solicitor may try to obtain an "ouster" against you. This is a court order telling you that you cannot live in your home and must leave.

- You should resist this as strongly as you can. If you suspect that your wife intends to demand an ouster, speak to your solicitor immediately.

- **Tell him that you intend to oppose this with every means you have. Ask him to explain all the ways he knows that you can resist.**

- **Here are some arguments that you can consider :**

    i) **It is your right to live in your home.** This is guaranteed by the Common Law ("An Englishman's home is his castle.") It is confirmed by the European Convention on Human Rights (Article 8) and the Human Rights Act 1998. You will seek very large compensation, in the European Courts, if your rights are abused.

    ii) **You have no-where else to live.** Your relatives will not have you. You cannot afford other accommodation and you cannot live on the street.

iii) **There is no reasonable cause to evict you.** You are no more to blame for any conflict in the home than your wife is. Perhaps she provokes conflict with the intention of having you evicted.

iv) **Your children need your presence in the home.** You are a stabilising influence on the household. It is your right and theirs' that you remain together.

v) **You cannot comply with an ouster order.** No court should make an order that someone cannot comply with. It is against natural justice.

vi) **If you are put in prison for not complying, your career is over.** You will not be able to return to your job. You and your family will become a permanent charge on public funds.

vii) **You will appeal to a higher court against any ouster order.** At the same time you will write the Department for Constitutional Affairs and your MP.

viii) **You will make an immediate appeal to the European Courts.** The "Stratagem" in "Tactics Masterclass" will be part of your appeal.

- Many men are outraged by the perversity and injustice of ouster orders. They prefer to spend some time in prison, rather than comply with the abuse of their fundamental human right to live in their home.

- Such men sit down in a chair and wait to be carried out. You may want to telephone the Press (local and national) if you think that you may be evicted.

DO NOT BE PROVOKED

- Your wife may attempt to provoke you into violence. This gives her an excuse to call the police and apply to a court for you to be evicted from your home.

- Do not be provoked. If she attacks you physically, gather evidence of this. Keep a written record of attacks, with the date, what happened and where. Keep the record at work or somewhere else that she cannot find it.

- See your doctor about any injuries or stress that you suffer. You can use a hidden tape recorder to record an attack or an admission by your wife that she does it.

- When you have convincing evidence, speak to your solicitor about going to the police. You can ask that your wife is prosecuted and removed from your home.

- See "Advanced Tactics" - A Violent Woman.

TACTICS IN COURT

Here are tactics to keep in mind whenever you get ready for any court hearing :

REPRESENT YOURSELF

- **You should always represent yourself in court. This has great advantages.** See "Represent Yourself" (on the Contents page).

- **You are entitled to represent yourself in any divorce court.**

- If you are ever asked why you are representing yourself, say that you cannot afford to bring a lawyer.

- Even if you have legal aid to pay for lawyers, this usually has to be paid back afterwards. The cost is large.

- Before a hearing, make notes of what you want to say (and consult your solicitor). At the hearing, always make a note of what is said.

- You can take a friend (who is not a solicitor) with you into court if you want to. He can make notes and speak to you quietly (but cannot explain your case to the judge). There is nothing to prevent you from taking a journalist as your friend, if you want to.

YOUR BEST STRATEGY

- **Your strategy will be a robust defence of your interests (and your children's welfare).**

  At the same time, you should not give a difficult judge an excuse to penalize you.

- **You should say bluntly what you want (and what is best for your children).**

  Do not be too aggressive, emotional or rude.

- None of this is difficult. Average common sense is all you need.

HOW THE COURT WORKS

- In most divorce courts, many of the "District" judges are only high street solicitors who work as part time judges. They do not have much training and are not particularly clever.

- In these courts there is only the judge and an "usher" (who shows you in).

- You and your wife's solicitor sit side by side at a table in front of the judge's table. Your wife will probably sit behind her solicitor.

- You can speak whenever the judge asks you to, or whenever he looks in your direction.

- Ask as many questions as you like. The judge has been told by his line managers to help anyone who represents himself. He must explain what is happening and must not allow you to be at a disadvantage.

YOU CAN BE BLUNT

- **It is your right, in any court, to say bluntly what you mean, in your own words.**

  Write down what you are going to say well before a hearing.

- Take care if you are aggressive, emotional or rude. If you express contempt for a judge or a court during a hearing, be prepared to be penalized.

- **You will be able to think of honest criticisms of your wife and the divorce system.**

  Here are some acceptable things that you can say :

  Your wife

  "This divorce is based on perjury. My wife's Petition contains lies. She is only concerned with stealing my property and has become a liar to get it. Giving her my property would be unlawful."

  "My wife has decided that she no longer wants me but is determined to steal my property. I will resist this through all the appeal courts."

  "I will not accept the unjust theft of my property (or the abduction of my children) just because that is what a selfish woman wants."

  "Of course keeping our home and looking after children is important. But it is not something that any decent person expects to be paid for."

  "No decent person demands forced payment for parenthood or sex."

  "My wife is putting her own interests before my children's welfare. She wants my basic rights destroyed. I do not expect an English court to reward her for selfishness, dishonesty and disloyalty."

  Your rights

  "This divorce system is abusing my rights to property, family life and fair treatment in a court open to Public and Press."

"I am angry at the injustice that is being done to me (and my children)."

"I resent the evil that is being done to me and my family."

"I will appeal against the injustice that is being done to me (and my children)."

"I will appeal if I am treated badly here."

"I will appeal."   "I will appeal."   "I will appeal."

The Divorce System

"Family courts that are held in secret, accept perjury and abuse fundamental rights to property and family life are against all the principles of British justice."

"I am horrified by a divorce system that encourages lying as a means of stealing an honest man's property and abducting his children."

"It is a dishonest divorce system that tries to prevent honest men from appealing against injustice by forcing their wife's costs onto them."

"Welfare Officers have a bad reputation. If they bully my children, or try to put words into their mouths, I will take action against them in the European Courts."

"This wicked divorce system must be reformed."

"What plans are there to reform these courts and give men justice?"

REPETITION REPETITION REPETITION

- Always repeat important points several times during a hearing.

- It is not enough to say something important only once, think of several different ways to say it. Write them all down when you make your notes before the hearing.

HAS THE JUDGE READ THE DOCUMENTS?

- **Make a list of the documents that are relevant to the hearing.**
  For example : your Answer to your wife's Petition may give important background information for all hearings.

- If you want to, you can write to the court manager a week before the hearing to say which documents you want the judge to read. Mark the letter "Urgent".

- When the hearing begins, ask the judge whether he has read each of these documents. If he has not, ask for an adjournment to another day, so that he can. Say that this should be at no cost to you.

- You are entitled to ask the judge a question to test whether he has read a document. For example : "Can I ask you whether you know my children's names and who looks after them on weekdays?"

- If a judge refuses to read any document that you think is relevant, say that this may make you appeal against all his decisions. Also say that, if a judge gives a document just a casual glance.

A RECORDING OF THE HEARING

- **Ask the judge whether an electronic recording is being made of the hearing.**

  If there is, you can ask for a typed copy. If you think that this is particularly important, write to the court manager before the hearing.

- This may be useful if you appeal. Also, the judge may treat your case more carefully if he knows that you will have a transcript.

- You are a taxpayer and should not be charged anything for this. If the judge demands an unreasonable fee, ask which law allows him to charge.

- If a recording is made but you are refused a typed copy, say that you will complain to the Secretary of State at the Department for Constitutional Affairs.

- You need the judge's agreement to use your own tape recorder for the hearing. If the judge refuses to allow you to use it, say "Justice should be seen and heard to be done". Ask to whom you should complain.

HOW MANY HEARINGS ?

- If you and your wife reach a voluntary agreement to have a divorce (and on finance, children and everything else), you may have only 1 or 2 hearings.

- If you decide to oppose her unreasonable demands, you may have 5 or 6.

- If you decide to appeal repeatedly against biased decisions by the unjust divorce courts, you may have 10 or 20 hearings or more.

- Do not forget that these unjust courts will try to force you to pay your wife's costs. They do this even when her divorce Petition is based on lies.

- If you are poor, or do not mind losing money (or have your money safe in a trust), you can keep divorce proceedings going for many years. This punishes both an unscrupulous wife and the unjust courts that encourage her.

- See "Costs" .

- See "Avoiding Her Costs" .

WHICH JUDGE ?

- There is usually no consistency in which judge you get for a hearing. If you have 10 hearings you may well get 10 different judges. This at least limits the damage that a particularly poor judge can do to you.

- If you like a particular judge, you can write to the court office (or telephone) a week before the next hearing. Ask for this judge to be given the case again. Say that the background is complicated and it will benefit everyone that he is already familiar with it.

IF YOU HAVE ANY DIFFICULTY

- If you have difficulty of any kind in court, say that you are representing yourself and cannot be expected to act like a lawyer. You expect special consideration and "direct assistance".

- The "Woolf Report" entitles you to this. You can ask the judge whether he has read this Report and say that you expect him to treat a "litigant in person" properly.

- See "Advanced Tactics" - "Dealing With a Difficult Judge".

EXPERT WITNESSES

- An expert witness is someone who claims to have specialist knowledge of something. They will come to court to support one side or the other, usually for a large fee (perhaps £1,000 for a day).

- Experts include: child psychologists, psychiatrists and property valuers.

- Their opinions are often not worth the hot air they express them with. But judges like them, because they give a judge a reason for favouring one side over the other.

- Your wife's solicitor must tell you well in advance of any hearing if she intends to produce an expert witness. If she springs one on you at the last moment, demand any adjournment at no cost to you, so you can decide if you need your own expert.

- If you are told that your wife will bring an expert to a hearing, consider whether you should find an expert to support you. They are expensive but, if you will be at a disadvantage without one, you may think it is worth the cost.

- If you decide to use one, find one who can be relied on to support what you want, who has years of experience in what he does, is articulate and respectable and has successfully appeared in court as an expert before.

- Consult your solicitor on whether you need one.

THE INFIGHTER'S GUIDE TO DIVORCE

- Recommend to every judge that he, and his colleagues, read **The InFighter's Guide to Divorce.**

- In future, there will be justice for men and children in "family" courts.

ADVANCED TACTICS

If you are determined to defend your interests vigorously, consider these more advanced tactics :

A "TACTICAL" ANSWER, APPEAL OR APPLICATION

- **<u>You must make an Answer to your wife's divorce Petition.</u>**

- **<u>This is vital whatever your plans for the future.</u>**

- **<u>A "tactical" Answer</u>** to a divorce Petition is one that you make to give you a negotiating position. You can withdraw it at any time in return for your wife agreeing a reasonable settlement (on finance, children and everything else) and to pay all her own costs.

- **You are entitled to make an appeal against any court order that you do not like.**

- **<u>A "tactical" appeal</u>** is one that you make with the intention of giving you a negotiating position. You can withdraw it at any time up to the court hearing if your wife agrees to something that you want and/or pays her own costs.

- **You are entitled to make an application for a court order against your wife if you want something from her.**

- **<u>A "tactical application"</u>** will cause delay and she may be prepared to pay her own costs or make some other concession if you agree to withdraw it.

- A "tactical" appeal or application may be more effective if you allow some time to pass before you offer to withdraw it. Do not tell anyone that your appeal or application is tactical. Always say that it is genuine.

- See "Contest the Divorce" .

- See "Avoiding Her Costs" .

DEALING WITH A DIFFICULT JUDGE

The best British judges do not want to work in the divorce courts because of the injustice and abuse of rights they inflict on men and children.

The tactics given here are to help you defend yourself when you meet a difficult judge. You can use some or all of them.

- **Appeal**

  If you think that you are being treated badly by a judge, say that you cannot accept injustice and you will appeal. You do not have to follow this through if you do not want to.

  You can say repeatedly : "I will appeal." "I will appeal." "I will appeal."

  Ask for the judge's full name, so that you can get the senior appeal judge to ask him to justify the injustice he has done you before the next hearing.

- **A Writ of Mandamus**

  This is an order by a higher court telling a junior judge he is wrong and must treat you properly.

  Tell the difficult judge that you will get one of these against him. Ask him to explain exactly what a writ of mandamus is and how you should apply for one. He is obliged to advise you.

  Consult your solicitor.

- **The Department for Constitutional Affairs**

  Tell the difficult judge that, if he does not treat you fairly, you will write to complain to the Secretary of State at the Department for Constitutional Affairs.

  Ask the judge for his full name and the Secretary of State's address.

  It is : Selborne House, 54-60 Victoria Street, London SW1E 6QW.

- **The European Courts**

  You can say : "If there is no justice for me in these terrible English courts, I will seek redress for the abuse of my rights in the European Courts. The British State will find it very expensive."

  Tell the judge he will have to go with you to Strasbourg or Luxembourg for the proceedings.

  See "Very Advanced Tactics" and "The European Courts" .

- **A Litigant in Person**

  If you have difficulty of any kind in a court, you can always say :

  "I am representing myself and the Woolf Report requires you to assist a litigant in person."

  You are entitled to special consideration and must not be put at a disadvantage.

- **An Adjournment**

  If you want to delay proceedings, ask for an adjournment, <u>without any cost to you</u>, so that you can consider legal representation. (You will probably only want to take your solicitor's advice.)

- **The Press and your MP**

  You can tell any judge that you intend to take any complaint about the way you are treated to the Press and your MP for action.

  You can email or write a letter to the editors of all major newspapers and news agencies.

- **No More Secret Courts**

  You can tell any judge that you do not approve of secret courts which keep out the Public and Press. They have a bad reputation for injustice all over the World.

  You want an adjournment so the Public and Press can be admitted and "injustice can be seen <u>not</u> to be done".

- **Complain to the Judge's Superior**

  You can say that you deeply resent the evil that is being done to you and your children. Ask for the name of the judge's superior so that you can make a written complaint.

- **Injustice**

  If any judge asks you what your grounds are for objecting to something, you can either give a detailed answer or you just reply "Injustice".

  You can say : "I will ask that, in future, you are not allowed to deal with any case where there are vulnerable children / complex financial issues / bad behaviour by a wife."

FIGHT TO THE END

- Look at what your wife is demanding. Also, ask your solicitor what he thinks your wife will get and what you will be left with after costs.

- If you will be left with little, you may want to fight on through many appeals. Legal costs will consume all your assets and there will be nothing left for your wife. You will at least have the satisfaction of not giving in to thievery and injustice.

- If the English courts try to stop you doing this, consider the European Courts. Consult your solicitor.

- See "European Courts".

A VIOLENT WOMAN

- Much domestic violence is started by women. If you have been a victim, write a detailed account of the attacks, with approximate dates. Type it, or write it neatly by hand.

- Gather as much evidence as possible. Photograph any injuries. If you have told friends or relatives, get written statements from them saying what they know.

- Consult your doctor about any harm that you have suffered, including bruising or stress. Get a letter from him confirming your injuries.

- Send a copy of this evidence to the court manager as soon as you have it. Attach a letter saying that you want it taken into account at all hearings.

- Before every hearing, write again to the court manager and say that you want the judge to read this evidence.

- At the beginning of each hearing, ask the judge if he has read it.

- **At any hearing about finance, say that you expect your wife to get much less money because of her violence. Say that her bad behaviour has been "<u>both obvious and gross</u>".**

- At any hearing about children, you can say that it is not safe for them to live with her, because she is violent.

NO MORE SECRET COURTS

- Write to the court manager before each hearing and ask that the Public and Press be admitted. Say that secret courts have a bad reputation for injustice throughout the world, and you do not want one.

- Scrutiny by the Press will make the judge much more careful to treat you properly. Say the same thing to the judge when you arrive at the hearing.

- Write to your MP and ask that no more divorce courts should be conducted in secret. You want him say this in Parliament.

- See "Your MP and MEP".

CONFRONT HER SOLICITOR

- You can get compensation from your wife's solicitor for bad practices.

- **Bad practices by her solicitor may include :**

  i) Failing to provide documents by a deadline set by a judge. This may mean that your wife may see documents that you have provided, before she sends her own. This gives her an unfair advantage.

ii) Back-dating letters, so that they appear to have been written before they were. Keep envelopes with post marks as evidence.

iii) Harassing you. For example: by persistently writing to ask you questions you have already answered.

- You can ask a judge to make a **"wasted costs order"** against any solicitor (or barrister) employed by your wife if :

  i) The solicitor acted improperly, unreasonably or negligently.

  ii) The solicitor's improper conduct has given you unnecessary costs.

  iii) Justice demands that, in all the circumstances, the solicitor should be ordered to compensate you for all or part of your costs.

- You can complain to the Law Society (**www.lawsoc.org.uk**) about harassment, dishonesty, malpractice or any other bad practice by your wife's solicitor. Particularly if you are representing yourself, as a "litigant in person".

- If the Law Society does not deal with your complaint to your satisfaction, complain about them to the Legal Services Ombudsman (**www.olso.org**).

- Ask for her solicitor's home address so that writs can be issued when she is not in her office. Tell her that her own private property is at stake in this case.

- Seek advice from your own solicitor. Listen carefully, but do not be easily discouraged by any reluctance by him to pursue a fellow lawyer.

A PERJURY LIST

- **Perjury is telling a lie in court or in any document written for a court. This is a criminal offence and can lead to prosecution.**

- Perjury is particularly serious if your wife does it to get your assets. That is **"perjury to facilitate fraud"**.

- Examine your wife's divorce Petition carefully for any false statement (and any other documents that she has provided for any court).

- If she has told lies, you should make a list of all her false statements. Get a copy of any documents that confirm this.

- You may want to use this in your negotiations with her. See "Negotiation". You can also say that you may send all the evidence you have to the Crown Prosecution Service, and ask for a criminal prosecution.

- Alternatively, you can send the list to the court. It is against the law that she should gain any benefit by committing a criminal offence. Ask for a suitable penalty and for her share of your assets to be substantially reduced as a result of her perjury.

- **Beware, if you think that your wife may be able retaliate by making a list of inaccuracies by you.**

VERY ADVANCED TACTICS

The tactics here are for you to use if you want to make a very robust defence of your interests (and those of your children).

Remember costs. Find out at the start what any costs will be.

GET REFERRED TO THE EUROPEAN COURT

- **The European Court of Justice** has the power to invalidate any English law that conflicts with European Union (EU) law or denies any of your rights.

- You can tell any English judge that you want him to refer your case to the European Court of Justice for a **"preliminary ruling"** on whether the English law he is using against you should be invalidated.

- Whenever an English judge forces a decision on you that you do not like, ask him which part of which English statute he is basing the decision on. You can say that this abuses your rights under EU law, including the **European Convention on Human Rights**.

INVALIDATE A BAD ENGLISH LAW

- You want a **"preliminary ruling"** to invalidate that English law. The Matrimonial Causes Act 1973, or any part of it, may be your target.

- If you can get the English judge to agree, it will be the British State that will be seeking clarification from the European Court of Justice on whether the English law conflicts with EU law.

- The European Court will not give a decision on your divorce case. But it can make void the bad English laws that are used to attack you and abuse your rights in the secret English divorce courts.

THIS COURT PROTECTS YOUR RIGHTS

- You can take part in the proceedings in the European Court of Justice, if you want to. The British State will pay most of the costs for the "preliminary ruling". Ask that they pay your costs for travel, accommodation and anything else.

- If you can get a bad English law knocked down by the European Court, then the English court dealing with your case must apply the European Court's declaration of your rights "without modification or distortion".

- If you are going to do this, get a copy of the **European Convention on Human Rights** and any other EU law you think is relevant to your case. Ask your solicitor to list all the English laws that may be used against you in the divorce courts.

YOU CAN DO IT YOURSELF

- If an English judge refuses to seek a "preliminary ruling", you can say that it is a serious matter for him to deny you this. He has no business to refuse a thorough examination of the law and he may be in contempt of the European Court of Justice.

- If he still refuses to refer your objection to an English law to the European Court, you can start proceedings in the European Court yourself if you want to.

  See "The European Courts" .

TACTICS MASTERCLASS

JUSTICE AT LAST

- The Stratagem given here is for use if you want to stop those attacking your rights and reform the unjust English courts that are being used against you.

- There are complex legal issues. You may want to ask your solicitor to find a lawyer experienced in the European Courts and constitutional matters to advise you.

- You should still continue to represent yourself when you can. But you should pay for some time with the specialist lawyer for expert advice. Remember costs. Find out, at the start, what they will be.

JUST SATISFACTION

- The European Court of Justice in Luxembourg is now the highest court with power in the United Kingdom. All English courts must do what it says.

- This Court has the power to invalidate Acts made by the Westminster Parliament. It can also stop unjust practices and the abuse of rights in all English courts.

- If any of your rights has been abused in an English court, you can apply to the European Court of Justice for **"just satisfaction"**.

- **"Just Satisfaction"** can include large financial compensation from the British State, the invalidation of bad English laws, and radical change to the English courts.

- See "The European Courts".

If you decide to go to the European Court of Justice, you may wish to include this Stratagem in your plea for Justice :

The European Court of Justice orders :

1. For their false judgements and abuse of rights:

   The forced resignation, without pension or gratuity, of all judges who have sat in the Family Division courts since 1973.

   This to include all British judges who have ever given judgement on any family matter during that time, including Law Lords.

2. For their neglect of rights and wretched ineptitude:

   The immediate and permanent closure of the Law Commission, whose function is to recommend reform of bad English laws.

   The annulment of the Law Commissions Act 1965.

3. The immediate restoration to all the men of the United Kingdom their rights to property, family life and fair treatment in open courts, guaranteed by the Common Law.

4. The European Convention on Human Rights to have <u>direct effect</u> in all courts of the United Kingdom, regardless of the Human Rights Act 1998 and other statutes.

5. The annulment of the Matrimonial Causes Act 1973 and all associated statutes.

   The Westminster Parliament to enact primary matrimonial legislation that complies with all rights under the Common Law and the European Convention on Human Rights. This legislation to be accessible to all and easy to understand.

6. The British State to pay exemplary damages to all citizens whose rights have been abused by a Family Division court since 1973.

EUROPEAN CONVENTION ON HUMAN RIGHTS

HUMAN RIGHTS ACT 1998

ANCIENT RIGHTS CONFIRMED

- **The European Convention on Human Rights, written in 1950, guarantees rights for everyone in the European Union, including the United Kingdom.**

  The document is also called the "Convention for the Protection of Human Rights and Fundamental Freedoms".

- The Convention is based on the United Nations' **"Universal Declaration of Human Rights"** written in 1948.

  The British Parliament made some Convention rights into English law, with the Human Rights Act 1998.

- **These all build on the ancient rights and liberties of the people of England under the Common Law; including the free enjoyment of personal security, personal liberty, private property and family life.**

- All the essential rights of the English people are confirmed to us, and firmly secured, by our ancient Common Law. There has never been any intention that the new international guarantees should supersede, or modify, our ancient rights.

DEMAND YOUR RIGHTS

- **No English court has any lawful authority to deny any of your fundamental rights or freedoms.**

- You can say to a judge: "I insist on my rights to property and family life under the Common Law and the European Convention on Human Rights. Any statute, or any court, that abuses my rights is illegitimate. It is an outrage against decency."

- See "Your Ancient Rights".

READ THIS IF YOU WANT TO

- **You do not have to read this. It is optional. If you are interested, the main Articles of the Convention are printed on the following pages.**

- You can get the full text of the Convention, if you want it, from **www.echr.coe.int**

  The Human Rights Act 1998 is on **www.opsi.gov.uk**

  Public libraries have both.

- If you read the following extract from the Convention :

  "The Court" is the European Court of Human Rights.

  "Just Satisfaction" includes large financial compensation that the Court can order the British State to pay to anyone whose rights, under the Convention, have been abused by an English court.

  "High Contracting Parties" are the governments of the countries belonging to the European Union, including the United Kingdom.

  "Protocols" are changes that have been made to the Convention. Some have been added into the main document; others are attached at the end.

- **The Articles of the Convention that are unlawfully violated every day in the English "family" courts are marked here by a line in the margin.**

CONVENTION FOR THE PROTECTION OF HUMAN RIGHTS AND FUNDAMENTAL FREEDOMS

Extract

Article 1 – Obligation to respect human rights

The High Contracting Parties shall secure to everyone within their jurisdiction the rights and freedoms defined in Section I of this Convention.

Section I – Rights and freedoms

Article 2 – Right to life

1   Everyone's right to life shall be protected by law. No one shall be deprived of his life intentionally save in the execution of a sentence of a court following his conviction of a crime for which this penalty is provided by law.

2   Deprivation of life shall not be regarded as inflicted in contravention of this article when it results from the use of force which is no more than absolutely necessary:

   a   in defence of any person from unlawful violence;

   b   in order to effect a lawful arrest or to prevent the escape of a person lawfully detained;

   c   in action lawfully taken for the purpose of quelling a riot or insurrection.

Article 3 – Prohibition of torture

No one shall be subjected to torture or to inhuman or degrading treatment or punishment.

Article 4 – Prohibition of slavery and forced labour

1   No one shall be held in slavery or servitude.

2   No one shall be required to perform forced or compulsory labour.

3   For the purpose of this article the term "forced or compulsory labour" shall not include:

   a   any work required to be done in the ordinary course of detention imposed according to the provisions of Article 5 of this Convention or during conditional release from such detention;

   b   any service of a military character or, in case of conscientious objectors in countries where they are recognized, service exacted instead of compulsory military service;

c   any service exacted in case of an emergency or calamity threatening the life or well-being of the community;

d   any work or service which forms part of normal civic obligations.

Article 5 – Right to liberty and security

1   Everyone has the right to liberty and security of person. No one shall be deprived of his liberty save in the following cases and in accordance with a procedure prescribed by law:

a   the lawful detention of a person after conviction by a competent court;

b   the lawful arrest or detention of a person for non-compliance with the lawful order of a court or in order to secure the fulfilment of any obligation prescribed by law;

c   the lawful arrest or detention of a person effected for the purpose of bringing him before the competent legal authority on reasonable suspicion of having committed an offence or when it is reasonably considered necessary to prevent his committing an offence or fleeing after having done so;

d   the detention of a minor by lawful order for the purpose of educational supervision or his lawful detention for the purpose of bringing him before the competent legal authority;

e   the lawful detention of persons for the prevention of the spreading of infectious diseases, of persons of unsound mind, alcoholics or drug addicts or vagrants;

f   the lawful arrest or detention of a person to prevent his effecting an unauthorized entry into the country or of a person against whom action is being taken with a view to deportation or extradition.

2   Everyone who is arrested shall be informed promptly, in a language which he understands, of the reasons for his arrest and of any charge against him.

3   Everyone arrested or detained in accordance with the provisions of paragraph 1.c of this article shall be brought promptly before a judge or other officer authorized by law to exercise judicial power and shall be entitled to trial within a reasonable time or to release pending trial. Release may be conditioned by guarantees to appear for trial.

4   Everyone who is deprived of his liberty by arrest or detention shall be entitled to take proceedings by which the lawfulness of his detention shall be decided speedily by a court and his release ordered if the detention is

not lawful.

5   Everyone who has been the victim of arrest or detention in contravention of the provisions of this article shall have an enforceable right to compensation.

Article 6 – Right to a fair trial

1   In the determination of his civil rights and obligations or of any criminal charge against him, everyone is entitled to a fair and public hearing within a reasonable time by an independent and impartial tribunal established by law. Judgment shall be pronounced publicly but the press and public may be excluded from all or part of the trial in the interests of morals, public order or national security in a democratic society, where the interests of juveniles or the protection of the private life of the parties so require, or to the extent strictly necessary in the opinion of the court in special circumstances where publicity would prejudice the interests of justice.

2   Everyone charged with a criminal offence shall be presumed innocent until proved guilty according to law.

3   Everyone charged with a criminal offence has the following minimum rights:

       a   to be informed promptly, in a language which he understands and in detail, of the nature and cause of the accusation against him;

       b   to have adequate time and facilities for the preparation of his defence;

       c   to defend himself in person or through legal assistance of his own choosing or, if he has not sufficient means to pay for legal assistance, to be given it free when the interests of justice so require;

       d   to examine or have examined witnesses against him and to obtain the attendance and examination of witnesses on his behalf under the same conditions as witnesses against him;

       e   to have the free assistance of an interpreter if he cannot understand or speak the language used in court.

Article 7 – No punishment without law

1   No one shall be held guilty of any criminal offence on account of any act or omission which did not constitute a criminal offence under national or international law at the time when it was committed. Nor shall a heavier penalty be imposed than the one that was applicable at the time the criminal offence was committed.

2   This article shall not prejudice the trial and punishment of any person for any act or omission which, at the time when it was committed, was

criminal according to the general principles of law recognized by civilized nations.

Article 8 – Right to respect for private and family life

1 Everyone has the right to respect for his private and family life, his home and his correspondence.

2 There shall be no interference by a public authority with the exercise of this right except such as is in accordance with the law and is necessary in a democratic society in the interests of national security, public safety or the economic well-being of the country, for the prevention of disorder or crime, for the protection of health or morals, or for the protection of the rights and freedoms of others.

Article 9 – Freedom of thought, conscience and religion

1 Everyone has the right to freedom of thought, conscience and religion; this right includes freedom to change his religion or belief and freedom, either alone or in community with others and in public or private, to manifest his religion or belief, in worship, teaching, practice and observance.

2 Freedom to manifest one's religion or beliefs shall be subject only to such limitations as are prescribed by law and are necessary in a democratic society in the interests of public safety, for the protection of public order, health or morals, or for the protection of the rights and freedoms of others.

Article 10 – Freedom of expression

1 Everyone has the right to freedom of expression. This right shall include freedom to hold opinions and to receive and impart information and ideas without interference by public authority and regardless of frontiers. This article shall not prevent States from requiring the licensing of broadcasting, television or cinema enterprises.

2 The exercise of these freedoms, since it carries with it duties and responsibilities, may be subject to such formalities, conditions, restrictions or penalties as are prescribed by law and are necessary in a democratic society, in the interests of national security, territorial integrity or public safety, for the prevention of disorder or crime, for the protection of health or morals, for the protection of the reputation or rights of others, for preventing the disclosure of information received in confidence, or for maintaining the authority and impartiality of the judiciary.

Article 11 – Freedom of assembly and association

1   Everyone has the right to freedom of peaceful assembly and to freedom of association with others, including the right to form and to join trade unions for the protection of his interests.

2   No restrictions shall be placed on the exercise of these rights other than such as are prescribed by law and are necessary in a democratic society in the interests of national security or public safety, for the prevention of disorder or crime, for the protection of health or morals or for the protection of the rights and freedoms of others. This article shall not prevent the imposition of lawful restrictions on the exercise of these rights by members of the armed forces, of the police or of the administration of the State.

Article 12 – Right to marry

Men and women of marriageable age have the right to marry and to found a family, according to the national laws governing the exercise of this right.

Article 13 – Right to an effective remedy

Everyone whose rights and freedoms as set forth in this Convention are violated shall have an effective remedy before a national authority notwithstanding that the violation has been committed by persons acting in an official capacity.

Article 14 – Prohibition of discrimination

The enjoyment of the rights and freedoms set forth in this Convention shall be secured without discrimination on any ground such as sex, race, colour, language, religion, political or other opinion, national or social origin, association with a national minority, property, birth or other status.

Article 15 – Derogation in time of emergency

1   In time of war or other public emergency threatening the life of the nation any High Contracting Party may take measures derogating from its obligations under this Convention to the extent strictly required by the exigencies of the situation, provided that such measures are not inconsistent with its other obligations under international law.

2   No derogation from Article 2, except in respect of deaths resulting from lawful acts of war, or from Articles 3, 4 (paragraph 1) and 7 shall be made under this provision.

3   Any High Contracting Party availing itself of this right of derogation shall keep the Secretary General of the Council of Europe fully informed of the measures which it has taken and the reasons therefor. It shall also inform the Secretary General of the Council of Europe when such measures have ceased to operate and the provisions of the Convention are again

being fully executed.

Article 16 – Restrictions on political activity of aliens

Nothing in Articles 10, 11 and 14 shall be regarded as preventing the High Contracting Parties from imposing restrictions on the political activity of aliens.

Article 17 – Prohibition of abuse of rights

Nothing in this Convention may be interpreted as implying for any State, group or person any right to engage in any activity or perform any act aimed at the destruction of any of the rights and freedoms set forth herein or at their limitation to a greater extent than is provided for in the Convention.

Article 18 – Limitation on use of restrictions on rights

The restrictions permitted under this Convention to the said rights and freedoms shall not be applied for any purpose other than those for which they have been prescribed.

Section II – European Court of Human Rights

Article 19 – Establishment of the Court

To ensure the observance of the engagements undertaken by the High Contracting Parties in the Convention and the Protocols thereto, there shall be set up a European Court of Human Rights, hereinafter referred to as "the Court". It shall function on a permanent basis.

Article 34 – Individual applications

The Court may receive applications from any person, non-governmental organisation or group of individuals claiming to be the victim of a violation by one of the High Contracting Parties of the rights set forth in the Convention or the protocols thereto. The High Contracting Parties undertake not to hinder in any way the effective exercise of this right.

Article 35 – Admissibility criteria

1 The Court may only deal with the matter after all domestic remedies have been exhausted, according to the generally recognized rules of international law, and within a period of six months from the date on which the final decision was taken.

2 The Court shall not deal with any application submitted under Article 34

that

a   is anonymous; or

b   is substantially the same as a matter that has already been examined by the Court or has already been submitted to another procedure of international investigation or settlement and contains no relevant new information.

3   The court shall declare inadmissable any individual application submitted under Article 34 if it considers that:

a   the application is incompatible with the provisions of the Convention or Protocols thereto, manifestly ill-founded, or an abuse of the right of individual application; or

b   the applicant has not suffered a significant disadvantage, unless respect for human rights as defined in the Convention and Protocols thereto requires an examination of the application on the merits and provided that no case may be rejected on this ground which has not been duly considered by a domestic tribunal.

4   The Court shall reject any application which it considers inadmissible under this Article. It may do so at any stage of the proceedings.

Article 41 – Just satisfaction

If the Court finds that there has been a violation of the Convention or the protocols thereto, and if the internal law of the High Contracting Party concerned allows only partial reparation to be made, the Court shall, if necessary, afford just satisfaction to the injured party.

Article 53 – Safeguard for existing human rights

Nothing in this Convention shall be construed as limiting or derogating from any of the human rights and fundamental freedoms which may be ensured under the laws of any High Contracting Party or under any other agreement to which it is a Party.

Protocol No. 1

Article 1 – Protection of property

Every natural or legal person is entitled to the peaceful enjoyment of his possessions. No one shall be deprived of his possessions except in the public interest and subject to the conditions provided for by law and by the general principles of international law.

The preceding provisions shall not, however, in any way impair the right of a State to enforce such laws as it deems necessary to control the use of property in accordance with the general interest or to secure the payment of taxes or other contributions or penalties.

Protocol No. 7

Article 5 – Equality between spouses

Spouses shall enjoy equality of rights and responsibilities of a private law character between them, and in their relations with their children, as to marriage, during marriage and in the event of its dissolution. This Article shall not prevent States from taking such measures as are necessary in the interests of the children.

Protocol No. 12

Article 1 – General prohibition of discrimination

1   The enjoyment of any right set forth by law shall be secured without discrimination on any ground such as sex, race, colour, language, religion, political or other opinion, national or social origin, association with a national minority, property, birth or other status.

2   No one shall be discriminated against by any public authority on any ground such as those mentioned in paragraph 1.

- The full text of the European Convention on Human Rights is on **www.echr.coe.int**

- See "Your Ancient Rights".

THE EUROPEAN COURTS

THE HIGHEST COURTS IN THE LAND

- **The highest courts with power in this country are now the European Courts.**

- All English courts, including the House of Lords, must do what the European Courts tell them.

- Any person who has had his rights abused in English courts can apply to a European Court for justice.

THERE ARE TWO EUROPEAN COURTS

- You have a choice of two courts. Which one you should write to depends on what has happened to you and what you want to do about it. You can apply to both at the same time if you want to.

The European Court of Human Rights

You can go to this court to get the violation of any of your rights stopped. Your rights are laid down in the document called the **"European Convention on Human Rights"**. See the previous Section. Your rights include: ownership of your property, and to bring up your children, and fair treatment in open courts.

The European Court of Justice

You apply to this court if you want any English law made invalid because it denies your rights or conflicts with a law of the European Union. One English law that you could seek to have invalidated is the Matrimonial Causes Act 1973, for the abuses of rights committed under it.

- There is no fee to apply to these courts and you can sometimes represent yourself if you want to. In some circumstances, you may need a lawyer.

- You may also take action in these courts on behalf of your children if their rights are violated by English courts.

THE EUROPEAN COURT OF HUMAN RIGHTS

IS THIS THE COURT FOR YOU ?

- **You must be able to show that one or more of your rights has been violated by an English court (or other official body). You are suing the British State for justice, not your wife.**

- This Court is in Strasbourg and you are entitled to submit an application by post. In most cases, there is no hearing. If there is, you can represent yourself at the Court if you want to. Proceedings are in English and the Court does not charge a fee.

- This is not a court of appeal which changes the decisions of English courts. But this Court has the power to force English courts to stop abusing rights. It can order large financial compensation for damage to you or your children.

WHICH OF YOUR RIGHTS HAS BEEN VIOLATED ?

- See the previous Section on the **"European Convention on Human Rights"** which lists your rights.

  The full text is on the Court's web site: **www.echr.coe.int**
  or get a copy from a public library.

- There have been 14 changes to the Convention over the years. These are called "protocols". Some have been incorporated into the document, others are attached at the end.

- **Decide which of your rights have been violated.**

  The most frequent violations in the English divorce courts are of :

  i) **Protection of Property   (Protocol 1, Article 1)**

     You are entitled to "the peaceful enjoyment of your possessions" and should not be deprived of them except for a powerful reason. Your wife's desire for a divorce is not an adequate reason.

ii) **Right to a Fair Trial   (Article 6)**

You are entitled to a fair, impartial hearing to which the Public and Press are admitted, so that justice is seen to be done. There should be no secret courts like the English divorce courts.

iii) **Right to Respect for Private and Family Life   (Article 8)**

You are entitled to enjoy a private life with your family in your home. This includes the right to live with and bring up your children. Your wife's preference to live apart is not an adequate reason to deprive you (and your children) of this.

iv) **Right to an Effective Remedy   (Article 13)**

You are entitled to an effective remedy in your own country against any violation of your rights and freedoms. There is no effective remedy in England against abuse of fundamental rights in the English divorce courts.

v) **Prohibition of Discrimination   (Article 14)**

You are entitled to your rights and freedoms without discrimination because of your sex or other status. The English divorce courts are infamous for their discrimination against men.

vi) **Equality between Spouses   (Protocol 7, Article 5)**

You are entitled to equality of rights and responsibilities during marriage, regarding children, and on divorce. Persistent discrimination against men denies you this.

WHEN TO APPLY TO THIS COURT

- **You can make an application to this Court as soon as any of your rights is violated.**

- The Court prefers you to wait until "all domestic remedies have been exhausted". **You can say that the English "family" courts are corrupt and there is no effective domestic remedy.** Also, you cannot afford the large fees charged by English courts like the House of Lords.

- An early application alerts this European Court to the abuse you are suffering and indicates that you will need their help in the future.

- You can tell any English judge that you have already put an application to the European Court. This may concentrate his mind on dealing with you more fairly.

- **If the European Court receives many applications like yours, it may persuade it to take action, at a high level, against injustice and abuse of rights in the English courts.**

- There is nothing to prevent you from sending the Court several applications on different violations. You can also resubmit the same application if it is rejected and then circumstances change, which they often do.

- You can withdraw an application at any time if you want to.

MAKING YOUR APPLICATION

- Get the "Application" form, the "Explanatory Note" and the "Rules of the European Court of Human Rights" from   **www.echr.coe.int** or your public library.

- **Complete the Application form. It should say that one (or several) of your rights has been violated. Say which rights and how they were violated. Attach any relevant documents.**

- You can include a copy of the article "Shameful and Despised", to give background, if you want to.

- **You must say these things in your application :**

  i)   **There is no effective remedy, or effective appeal, in England.**

  ii) **The "exhaustion of domestic remedies rule" has been satisfied.**

  iii) **You are sending your application within 6 months of a decision that violated your rights.**

  iv) **You want the European Court to stop the abuse of rights by which English courts have done damage to you (and your children). Say what you want.**

- You can claim large financial compensation from the British State for ruining your life. Do not ask for less than one million €uros (and all your costs since legal proceedings began).

- Send your application to :

  The Registrar
  The European Court of Human Rights
  Council of Europe
  F- 67075 Strasbourg
  Cedex
  France

- Send an email, or a paper copy, to the national press if you want publicity.

WHAT HAPPENS NEXT

- **Court officials decide whether your application is admissible and say if the Court will consider it.**

- The Court will probably deal with your case just by writing to you. They may ask for further information and ask you to say what **"just satisfaction"** (redress and compensation) you want from the British State. Ask for large financial compensation (and for the British State to pay your expenses).

- Hearings are rare. Your case will almost certainly be dealt with entirely by post. You will not therefore need to go to Strasbourg. But ask for a hearing if you want one.

- Your case will be dealt with free of charge by the Court.

- You are liable only for the expenses you have incurred yourself. The Court may give you Legal Aid for lawyer's fees if you cannot afford them. Find out if you will have to pay any of it back, before you accept.

- **A decision by the European Court in your favour is binding on the British Government and all English courts.**

NO ENGLISH JUDGE CAN INTERFERE

- No English judge can stop, or delay, you making an application to the European Court of Human Rights.

- The European Convention on Human Rights, Article 34, forbids the British State to "hinder in any way" your right to go to the European Court.

- You can say to an English judge :

  "You have no business to interfere with my right to go to the European Courts."

  "You are prohibited from interfering and there will be serious trouble if you do."

THE EUROPEAN COURT OF JUSTICE

The European Court of Justice is the highest court in Europe.

All English courts must do what it says.

IS THIS THE COURT FOR YOU ?

- **You can apply to this Court if you want a bad English law invalidated. That law can then no longer be used against you or anyone else.**

- **Any law that you denounce must be one that is of "direct and individual concern" to you. You must be a victim of this law.**

- **You can ask the Court to tell an English court to compensate you for any damage you have suffered as a result of a bad English law.**

- This Court is in Luxembourg. You are entitled to make an application by post. A hearing, if there is one, will be in English and the Court does not charge a fee.

- In some proceedings you can represent yourself, in others you must ask your solicitor (or another lawyer) to do it.

WHAT IS THIS COURT FOR ?

- **The European Court of Justice protects the individual against the State. It upholds EU law, our rights and fundamental freedoms.**

- The European Court of Justice has the power to make a "violation judgement" against any Act of Parliament, or other English statute, that is unjust and conflicts with any right guaranteed by European Union law.

- Your main rights and freedoms are listed in the document called **"The European Convention on Human Rights".**
  See the previous Section above.

- You can get the full text from **www.echr.coe.int**   or from a public library.

- Many other rights are given to us in other European Union laws. See below.

- **If The European Court of Justice issues a "violation judgement" against a bad English law, the British Parliament must decide how the bad law should be struck down.**

- You <u>cannot</u> appeal to this Court against a bad decision made against you in an English divorce court. <u>This is not a court of appeal.</u>

- But you can ask it to invalidate bad English laws, stop unjust court procedures and order an English court to compensate you.

WHAT YOU CAN ASK THE COURT TO DO FOR YOU

- **You can ask The European Court of Justice to :**

  i) **Invalidate an English law (or part of it) that was used to make a bad decision against you personally (or your children) because "EU law precludes this type of English law".**

  ii) **Demand change in the way that an English law you are a victim of is applied.**

  iii) **Propose change, or closure, of any part of the English legal system that has denied or abused your rights.**

  iv) **Compensate you for injustice you have suffered from a bad law by ordering the British State to pay you large damages. This is called "just satisfaction".**

- You might, for example, start an action in the European Court of Justice to invalidate a law (or several laws) relevant to your divorce proceedings.

- You could then ask the English divorce court to adjourn its proceedings until the European Court has decided whether to invalidate these laws. This takes about 18 months.

- If you want to do this, you should ask your solicitor to give you a list of the English laws relevant to your divorce proceedings. This will include the Matrimonial Causes Act 1973.

- The Court's website is : www.curia.eu.int/en/index.

WHAT IS EUROPEAN UNION LAW ?

- **The European Union has made its own laws.** They are called EU law, or EC law, or Community law. These laws apply in all EU countries including the UK.

- **EU laws are "superior" to English statutes.** If an English statute conflicts with an EU law, English courts must use the EU law. The European Court of Justice can tell them to abandon that English statute.

- **European Union Law is made up of :**

  i) **Treaties**

     Agreements signed by the countries that make up the European Union. All EU law is based on these Treaties. There are a large number of them.

  ii) **Directives**

     Instructions by the European Union to the British Parliament (and other EU parliaments) to make a law to achieve an objective.

  iii) **Regulations**

     These instructions are made by the European Union and apply in all English courts without the need for the Westminster Parliament to make a law.

  iv) **Decisions**

     These are specific instructions to particular countries, organisations or individuals to do something (or not do it).

  v) **Case Law**

     These are cases decided by the European Court of Justice in the past. These may show how your case might be treated if you go to the Court now.

- Many of these laws confer rights on all European citizens which English courts must uphold.

- These websites give the text of EU law documents in English :

  i) **www.europa.eu.int/eur-lex**

     EUR-Lex holds some EU Treaties and other documents. It is free.

  ii) **www.europa.eu.int/celex**

      CELEX is the most complete database of EU law up to December 2004. It is free.

YOUR RIGHTS HAVE BEEN ABUSED

- **When you apply to this Court, you must say that one (or more) of your rights under EU law has been abused by the British State.**

- Produce a list from your solicitor of all the English laws relevant to your divorce proceedings. Decide which you want invalidated.

- **You can say that those English laws infringe your rights under :**

  i) **The European Convention on Human Rights, and**

  ii) **All provisions in EU Treaties, directives and regulations that protect the right to property, fair trial, private and family life, effective remedy in law, non-discrimination and equality between spouses.**

- If you want to, you can read through the EU Treaties, directives, regulations, decisions and case law. Identify exactly which rights in these laws have been abused in your own case. State these EU laws (and your rights that have been abused) in your application to the Court.

- **You can say that you want the European Court of Justice to tell the Westminster Parliament and English courts that England must have a divorce system and family courts that the men of this country can accept.**

MAKING YOUR APPLICATION

- You should type, or write, your application to the Court on A4 paper.

- **Your application should give this information :**

  i)   Your name and address.

  ii) Your solicitor's name, address, telephone number, fax number and email address. Confirmation that he is authorized to practice in English courts.

  iii) Who you are making your application against. This will probably be the British State and the English courts of the Family Division.

  iv) What you are complaining against and a summary of your reasons and arguments. Say whether you want a hearing.

  v)   The order you want the Court to make to correct injustice, including any English laws you want invalidated.

  vi) The damages that you want from the British State for ruining your life. You can ask the Court to award you "exemplary damages". Do not ask for less then one million €uros (and all your costs since legal proceedings began).

  vii) The nature of the evidence supporting your application.

- Attach all the documents that support your application and a list of these documents. The Court needs 5 complete copies and a copy for anyone else who may have an interest.

- Every copy should be dated and signed by you and your solicitor.

- **Send your application to :**

The Registrar
The Court of Justice of the European Communities
L-2925
Luxembourg

WHAT HAPPENS NEXT

- **Court officials will decide whether the Court will consider your application.** If it is admissible, they will send a copy to the British State and anyone else interested.

- **Those interested have a month to comment.** You can then comment on what they have said and send the Court any further evidence.

- **A Court with several judges will deal with your case.** One judge, is called the **"Judge-Rapporteur"**. He will read all the papers in detail and advise the other judges whether inquiries are needed.

- **The judges will also take advice from an official called an "Advocate General".** His job is to read the papers, summarize the evidence and give an independent opinion on your case.

THE HEARING & THE JUDGEMENT

- **The Court will decide whether a hearing in Luxembourg is needed.** (You should say if (and why) you want any witnesses there. You may have to pay their expenses in advance.) The main emphasis is on the written submissions, and any hearing will be relatively short.

- **You may have to be represented at a hearing by your solicitor (or other lawyer or adviser).** All parties can ask to question any witness.

- **The Judges will give their judgement at a hearing.** The judgement is binding on everyone, including the British State and the English courts.

LEGAL AID & COSTS

- **You can apply to the Court for Legal Aid for all (or part) of your costs for the proceedings.** You can apply at any time and do not have to go through a lawyer.

- You must say why you cannot pay yourself and send evidence. You must send a document from a "competent authority" certifying your lack of means.

- **If you apply for Legal Aid, ask at the beginning whether you must pay any of it back.**

- The Legal Services Commission, in London, may also help you to obtain Legal Aid for court proceedings in Europe. Contact them on tel: 020 7759 0000.

- **The Court can order any unsuccessful party to pay the lawyers' bills and expenses of another. If the British State intervenes in a case it must pay its own costs.**

- **Get the Court officials to say clearly, at the beginning, what you would be liable for if you do not win.**

THE EUROPEAN COMMISSION MAY DO IT FOR YOU

- **The European Commission is a powerful body. It is there to help you if the British State abuses your rights and treats you unjustly.**

- You can of course make an application direct to the European Court of Justice yourself if you want to. Alternatively, you can approach the European Commission and ask them to apply to the Court for you.

- If you want the Commission to do it for you, you can either :

  i) Write to them on A4 paper. Say how your rights have been abused and give the information listed in "Making Your Application" above.

  or

  ii) Complete the Commission's complaint form, which you get from **http://europa.eu.int/comm/sg/lexcomm**

- If the Commission helps you, you can ask them whether you can represent yourself at the European Court of Justice.

- **The Commission's address is :**

  The Secretary-General
  Commission of the European Communities
  Rue de la Loi 200
  B-1049 Brussels
  Belgium

ADVICE FROM A SPECIALIST

- If you want to, you (or your solicitor) can find a lawyer who has experience of the European Court of Justice. Pay for an hour of his time for advice on :

    i)   The best way to present your case.

    ii)   How your application to the Court can be strengthened,

    iii)   Which European Union laws are relevant and the English statutes you might want invalidated, and

    iv)   Which precedents you can use.

- Tell him that you are representing yourself and want to do as much of the work as possible.

- See "Very Advanced Tactics" and "Tactics Masterclass" .

YOUR MP AND MEP

WRITE TO YOUR MP (and MEP)

- New divorce laws are needed and your Member of Parliament (and Member of the European Parliament) can start this reform.

- Get their names by telephoning a local political party office.

- **Write to your MP at :**

  The House of Commons,
  London SW1A 0AA.

- **Write to your Member of the European Parliament at :**

  The European Parliament,
  47-53 Rue Wiertz - Wierzstraat,
  B-1047 Brussels,
  Belgium.

- **In each letter, say that you want him to take the lead in Parliament to have new divorce laws made. Say that this is urgent.**
  To start this action, you want him to write to the appropriate ministers.

- **Tell him that the divorce courts are corrupt because :**

  i)   **An unlawful system of divorce on demand exists. It is used to abuse men's basic rights to property and parenthood under the European Convention on Human Rights, the Human Rights Act 1998 and the Common Law of England.**

  ii)   **Perjury (telling lies in court) by women demanding divorce is accepted by English judges every day. False judgements are common.**
        This is their normal basis for business.

  iii) **Theft of the property of honest men is the incentive for women to destroy their families.**
        This is why 70% of divorces are now sought by women.

  iv)   **Children are seized from their fathers.**
        To deny men the right to bring up their children is a gross abuse of men's rights.

v) **Children are denied the right to a stable and secure home with their father.**
This is a gross abuse of children's rights. 150,000 children go through the divorce courts every year. Most are damaged for the rest of their lives.

vi) **Secret courts are always unjust.**
The Press and Public are not allowed into most divorce courts. Without scrutiny there is always injustice. Fair trial, in open court, is an ancient English right. All courts should be open to all, whether those involved ask for it or not. Injustice must be seen <u>not</u> to be done.

vii) **The Legal Aid system discriminates against men.**
Men in work are usually refused Legal Aid and they cannot claim costs from a wife who has it. A wife has a bottomless purse to pay lawyers, while her husband is impoverished.

viii) **Inflated lawyers' bills are forced onto men to deter them from appealing against injustice.**
A wife's lawyers are allowed to more than double their bill whenever the husband is made to pay her costs.

- Your MP (or MEP) may say that he cannot interfere with your court case. Do not be put off by this. You are asking him to start reform in Parliament, which is his job.

- Say that the reform of the corrupt divorce courts is the most important human rights issue in this country today. The fundamental rights of men and children have been abused for more than a generation.

- This is the most important political reform that he should be concerned about. You want him to take action in Parliament immediately.

- In addition to your own MP (& MEP) you can write to as many others as you like. Start with well-known ones. Send them all an email if you want to. Their email addresses are on **www.parliament.uk**

- See the example of a letter to your MP (or MEP) in Annex 13.

THE 9 PRINCIPLES FOR REFORM

Reform of the unjust divorce courts, to stop the frivolous and dishonest pursuit of divorce, is now urgent.

The Performance Indicator for new legislation and procedures will be that :

i) The divorce rate in the United Kingdom will fall by 33%.

ii) The percentage of all divorces obtained by women (now 70%) will fall to below 50%.

Reform will include these Principles :

PRINCIPLE 1

Financial incentive to divorce will cease.

The enrichment of women seeking divorce will be substantially reduced.

PRINCIPLE 2

The division of assets on divorce will be in the proportions that the parties contributed to the marriage, with some provision where this would result in considerable hardship.

PRINCIPLE 3

Where there is a net transfer of assets from one party to another on divorce, the total assets to be taken away by the beneficiary will not exceed one third of the total assets of the couple.

Pensions will be excluded from the calculation of all settlements.

Needlessly large settlements will cease.

PRINCIPLE 4

There will be a financial clean break in all divorces, with no continuing enforced liability by either party for the other, except in the most exceptional circumstances.

The Performance Indicator will be: continued liability in less than 5% of divorces.

PRINCIPLE 5

The presumption will be that, after divorce or separation, children will reside with the parent who made the greater effort to prevent divorce and keep the family together.

Children will be entirely maintained by the family in which they live.
Child support maintenance by an absent parent will be entirely voluntary.

PRINCIPLE 6

Unreasonable Behaviour as grounds for divorce will be replaced by Cruelty.

Adultery will only be grounds for divorce when supported by Desertion, Separation or Cruelty.

PRINCIPLE 7

Reform of Legal Aid provision will ensure that where one party in a divorce gets Aid so will the other.

PRINCIPLE 8

No Respondent in divorce proceedings shall be required to pay any of the Petitioner's costs.

PRINCIPLE 9

There will be no more secret courts.

All court proceedings dealing with divorce and other family matters will be open to the Public and the Press, whether the parties want this or not.

Reporting restrictions will be minimal.

SHAMEFUL AND DESPISED

The Abomination of England's Secret Courts

There is a human rights issue in Britain today that transcends all others. It is an abuse of human rights on a huge scale and has endured for more than a generation. The most fundamental human rights of honest citizens are attacked every day and there is no redress. The British State is the perpetrator of this abuse and future historians will look back aghast that this scandal could happen in Britain.

The venue for this abuse of human rights is a system of secret courts which extends across the country. These courts are closed to the Public and do not permit scrutiny by the Press. Only those inside the organisation that runs the courts know exactly what happens in them. Like all secret courts they preserve their secrecy to conceal great harm and injustice to their victims. These are Divorce Courts.

Secret courts have a bad reputation for perverting justice wherever they are used in the world and it is shameful that they are now active here. But the divorce industry closely guards its secrecy. With scrutiny of its activities prevented, there is little public understanding of what it does to men and their children.

Injustice in the Divorce Courts takes different forms. The ancient Common Law rights of men to the peaceful enjoyment of their own property, to parenthood and fair treatment in open courts are denied. Guarantees of these rights under the European Convention on Human Rights are ignored. Perjury by women seeking divorce is now accepted legal practice in British courts. Theft, by divorce, of the property of blameless men is the daily business of these courts. Children are taken from their fathers against the will of both men and children. This sordid injustice gives the United Kingdom the highest divorce rate in Western Europe, 50% above the average. It is plain that all this could not happen without the compliance of the judiciary at the highest level. The whole of the British legal systems is tainted by these shameful, little courts.

The current law requires that a divorce is only granted if there has been adultery, desertion, separation or unreasonable behaviour. There is no lawful basis for divorce on demand. But the duplicity of the Divorce Courts is such that they do not apply the law as Parliament intended. Women seeking to dispose of a husband most often allege his "unreasonable behaviour" as grounds for divorcing him. These allegations frequently contain lies or exaggerations and many wives' lawyers encourage deception. Judges wink at this falsehood. Even though a wife may put lies in her divorce petition, it will seldom do her husband any good to tell the truth. The presumption is that she will get her divorce, and in most cases seize most of his property, whatever the circumstances. Tolerance of perjury, on a large scale, to attack honest men is the antithesis of what any justice system should be about.

So keen are the courts to grant divorce that even a woman who is severely mentally ill, and whose mental state is disturbed by psychotropic drugs, will be given legal aid and offered large financial incentives to dissolve her family. The Divorce Courts have no interest in stopping, or even delaying, such cases. At the same time, the courts will show a strong preference for requiring children to live with a mentally ill woman rather than with a normal, rational husband. The potentially disastrous consequences of the break up of a family under these circumstances are seen as no obstacle to giving the woman what she wants. At the same time, it is certain that the man will be made to finance the problems created by this meddlesome bureaucracy to the limit of his capacity.

In the United Kingdom today, there are 160,000 divorces a year and over 40% of marriages end this way. 70% of divorces are now obtained by women. The main reason that women now find divorce so attractive is the large financial rewards that the court system offers to most wives if they choose to abandon their husband. Many billions of pounds a year are now seized from husbands by deserting wives. The cry that rings through the Divorce Courts is "I don't want my husband - but I want his money". The financial prospects of a man who marries (and is then divorced), and a man who never lives with a woman, now diverge dramatically. It is a tribute to the decency and loyalty of half the women in this country that they remain with their husbands when such prizes are offered to them. Nevertheless, the annual number of marriages has fallen by 23% in the last decade, as the State has made marriage an increasingly onerous burden for men.

An ordinary man of average means taken to these courts will loose far more than half his property. On average, a man brings several times as much asset value into a marriage as the woman, but on divorce it is usually the woman who takes away much more than the man. He will be forced to pay the bill from his wife's lawyers, who are allowed to double their legal aid charges when a husband pays. Many men have walked away from the Divorce Courts stripped of all their property. Pensions are also seized and future income taken as maintenance. This plunder can then be used to finance the abduction of a man's children. There is no precedent in recent British history for the confiscation of property on this scale or the enforced removal of children from their parent. To steal most or all of a man's property, and his children, is to take away everything that is important to him. To force him to continue to finance his former wife, in circumstances to which he is bitterly opposed, is a condition close to slavery.

When men marry, few understand the destructive consequences of divorce, both for their long term financial well being or for their right to be a parent to their children. Divorce for men is highly damaging, whereas for women there are frequently very large, immediate benefits. Many divorced women are materially much better off than if they had remained single, whereas men who are divorced are invariably much worse off. Many men, who have worked productively all their lives, will find that they have very little at the end of it. Most men attacked in this way have done no significant wrong and both they, and their children, are victims of a most unjust and unprincipled divorce system, which scorns their fundamental rights. For a generation, millions of men and millions of children have suffered the treachery of these closed courts.

Only in the last half century have most ordinary men, by their own efforts, acquired substantial assets. At the same time, the predatory divorce system has grown up to steal from them. A deserting wife, who rattles her begging bowl in the Divorce Courts, now expects to strip her husband of his property, regardless of her own financial contribution to the marriage, and regardless of her own behaviour. Assets are divided on a "no fault" basis, which means that a woman who is entirely to blame for the end of a marriage can still expect to seize most or all of her husband's property. Without this unearned enrichment of women, many divorces sought by women would not happen. For courts to proffer payment for dishonestly breaking a contract, whether a marriage contract or any other, is a serious distortion of justice.

A man who represents himself in these Divorce Courts may find that he is the only man there. He may be confronted by a female judge, a female usher, a female barrister, a female solicitor, a female clerk and his wife. He is left in no doubt by these women's courts that their purpose is to steal most of the possessions for which he has spent his life working. These petticoated harpies have no interest in his rights to his own property, his old age pension, his future income or in his right to bring up his children. The unearned enrichment of the woman is what these unscrupulous courts are about and all else is secondary. No man would go into these courts if it were not for the threat of juridical violence against him, which underpins everything they do.

For most of the last century, communists of different kinds demanded that the private property of men must belong to the "collective". Now it is feminists and their fellow travellers who want it for women. Men's property must not belong to the individual, it must be "marital". Both creeds attack the freedom and integrity of the individual, which is the basis of civilized life, and both are immensely destructive. The Marxist ethic caused terrible injustice and destroyed wealth wherever it was imposed. Now the extremes of feminism, and theft by divorce, have equally serious consequences. This attack is not only on the vital interests of the individual but also on the natural family of father, mother and children, which is the social unit of all stable and successful societies. The greatest and lasting damage, done by the excesses of the divorce industry, is to children for whom it means the collapse of their family and the traumatic end to the security of a stable home.

The assault on children's interests is aided by "welfare officers" employed by the Divorce Courts to investigate families and recommend what should happen to children. Cynical lip service is paid by these people to the interests of children in divorce cases. They say that the interests of children are put first, but this is humbug. The reality is that children are usually treated as the property of their mother. Children are bullied, pressured, and words put into their mouths, by these "welfare officers", to persuade them to agree that they wish to live with their mother after her divorce. This outrage happens even when the woman is mentally ill or violent. The children's need for a home and maintenance is then used as a further argument for seizing the husband's property for his wife. The preoccupation of Divorce Court judges is to finance the otherwise financially unviable domestic unit of unmarried mother and children.

The main purpose of modern marriage is the provision of a secure and stable home for children until they are able to fend for themselves. The purpose is not to indulge the self interest of either the man or the woman. Yet 150,000 children are damaged every year by a divorce system that places parental preferences above children's essential interests. Adults are encouraged to childish self-interest, while children have the cares of adults forced on them. The effect on children of a broken home is permanent. Children whose family is pulled apart suffer many disadvantages. On average they have lower educational achievements and a higher tendency to crime than those who live with both parents. They are also more likely to be divorced themselves in the future. A plague of fatherless families will have far reaching destructive effects on the social fabric of this country long into the future.

Child rearing is one of the most demanding and important activities that most people do. For many of us it is the only legacy that we leave behind at the end of our lives. It is difficult enough to achieve the best for our children, even when there are two parents working together. No sole parent, however determined, can make the effort and input of two. Also, a father's influence on his children's development is irreplaceable, and is something that the mother cannot make herself, however good she is as a mother. A father's presence contributes uniquely to his children's sense of identity, self worth, esteem and responsibility to others. The continual parental attention that comes from the father's permanent presence at home is vital to the proper development of any child's personality. Similarly, of course there is a unique input by a mother that a father cannot make. It may also be true that many women are better as mothers when living with their children's father.

Young children who live without their natural father are more likely to suffer both physical and mental ill health, including depression and low self-esteem. Such children are more prone to problems at school, poor academic performance and conflict with teachers. Hostility and anti-social behaviour towards adults and authority is particularly prevalent in boys who grow up without their natural father. A significant threat to a child comes from the absence of the natural father and his replacement in the home with another man who is not married to the child's mother. Different studies indicate that the risk of fatal abuse to a child is many times greater in a step-family than if the child lives with both natural parents. Yet it is exactly this deleterious development that the divorce system facilitates. A child's natural father is, and always has been, the child's most effective provider and protector, and his forced exclusion from the family can be damaging to the child in many ways.

Teenagers of divorced parents continue to suffer difficulties from childhood and, for them the problems and pitfalls of adolescence are exacerbated. Precocious sexual encounters for both boys and girls mean that they are almost twice as likely to become teenage parents as they would if their own parents had remained together. They are at least 50% more likely to smoke or take drugs and young men are 60% more likely to persistently break the law than teenagers from intact two parent families. Young people living with a lone mother are three times more

140

likely to be excluded from school and twice as likely to leave school with no qualifications. The teenager whose home has been broken is more inclined to aggressive and delinquent behaviour and is emotionally vulnerable. The direct causes include lack of parental attention and a less stable and disciplined home life.

The lasting damage done to children and teenagers by the turbulence of divorce persists into adulthood. Young adults whose parents have divorced are more likely to be unemployed and to have low incomes. They have a higher incidence of physical and mental ill health and of alcohol abuse. Young men from broken families have not had the mature example of their own father and mother living together and co-operating for the benefit of their family. As a result they are significantly more likely to dissolve their own first partnership. Both young men and women whose parents divorced are twice as likely to have their first child outside marriage, or stable cohabitation, as those who grew up with both their natural parents.

There are serious consequences for society in failing to nurture the next generation. A great weight of evidence shows that the best environment for bringing up children is the family based on the marriage of their natural father and mother. The collapse of a family frequently leads to poverty and hardship, emotional distress and a bleaker future for all its members. The damage to children is reflected in society's ills. Research in Britain and abroad consistently shows that divorce and fatherlessness are major contributors to low living standards, poor educational achievement and economic decline. Criminal activity, persistent reoffending and higher rates of child homicide are all closely linked to the domestic instability caused by mass divorce.

The engine driving these profound social changes is the dismal bureaucracy of the divorce industry. This comprises judges, lawyers, "welfare officers" and other bureaucrats, for whom marriage is only a vehicle for transferring assets from men to women. The imbalance and injustice of a divorce system by which 70% of divorces are obtained by women, frequently seeking enrichment, is obvious to these bureaucrats. Yet they treat with distain the right of men to the peaceful enjoyment of their own property, or to bring up their children; and regard perjury as an acceptable basis for business. These bureaucrats have swallowed so much of the extremes of feminism that, what they suppose are the interests of women, must be pursued, no matter how destructive to society or harmful to individuals. The denial of essential individual freedom and the rights of ordinary men and their children, by secret courts, has become the most important human rights issue in this country for over a hundred years.

Marriage has been one of our most valuable social creations and its steady decline is a tragedy that should not have happened. The attack by the British State on the family, private property and the vital interests of children has been done without the consent of the majority of the people and, to a large extent, without their knowledge. There has been no popular demand for this travesty of decency. Clearly, a significant minority of women do support the confiscation of men's property, and the exclusion of men from child rearing, or they would not accept the State's offer to coerce and rob their husbands. But these abuses are fiercely resisted by nearly all men and opposed by many women. Few grandmothers who have seen their sons financially ruined, and separated from their children, regard the forced promotion of fatherless families by the State with anything but horror.

The divorce bureaucracy usually ignores criticism and does not trouble to defend its actions. When it does respond, it is with the claim that the decline of marriage and the family only reflects processes "deep in the fabric of society". This is facetious pretence. They understand well enough that the large financial incentives that they offer for women to divorce, and the consistent awarding of child custody to women, are major factors in encouraging mass divorce. It is deliberate and wilful deception for Divorce Court judges and bureaucrats to pretend that the current law, and the way it is applied, are not the direct cause of the highest divorce rate in Western Europe. Comfortable with perjury, oblivious to their abuse of men's rights to property and parenthood, these amoral servants of the State carelessly inflict terrible damage on our children. The deep resentment and contempt felt by most men, for a court system that has lost its way, will itself have far reaching consequences.

Our lack of vigilance to protect our most important rights has cost the men and children of this country dear. While the good have neglected public affairs, the bad and the foolish have dismantled essential rights and freedoms. The remedy for this disastrous state of affairs must be radical. Restoration of the natural family, marriage and individual property rights is urgent. It is central to achieving this that the financial incentives for women to divorce must be substantially reduced. Judges must also be cured of their irrational belief that a man cannot have custody to care for children when his wife wishes to dissolve their family. Primary legislation is essential and the discretionary powers of divorce judges, who have shown without doubt that they cannot be trusted, must be severely curtailed. The tainted judges of the Family Division can have no part in a reformed system. They will be dismissed.

The target for the legislators must be to reduce divorces obtained by women from over 70% to below 50%. When the financial incentives that come from the seizure by deserting wives of their husband's property are removed, the divorce rate will fall very substantially. The presumption must be that, when divorce happens, children will remain with the parent who has most assiduously tried to keep their family together. The immense damage that divorce does in this country will then be significantly reduced. New legislation must be based on the civilising values of a proper regard for men's property and the protection of children within their natural family. The parliamentarians who have ignored the appalling abuse of human rights for over a generation must be stirred from their lethargy.

For as long as the shameful and despised little Divorce Courts continue as they are, so long will the reputation of this part of the British legal systems lie in the gutter. We used to be so proud of British Justice. How did it come to this?

FORWARD PLANNING

TO MARRY OR NOT TO MARRY

- **First, you will want to consider whether marriage is best for you.**

- Marriage is one of our most valuable social creations. It is the foundation of all stable and prosperous societies. A great weight of evidence shows that children thrive best in the family of their married parents.

- But, the British State has now attacked the institution of marriage for more than a generation.

- **For men, marriage has been made an onerous burden, and divorce (or separation) financially ruinous. Think carefully.**

BE PREPARED

- **Divorce is now the most ruinous ordeal to which an honest man can be subjected in this country. It is often entirely undeserved.**

- Just as we plan for other disasters in life, with insurance and similar contingencies, we must protect ourselves from the wickedness of the detested divorce courts.

- It is possible to reduce the damage that divorce courts can do you, by planning your finances, and other affairs, before your wife decides to divorce you.

- **If you put your assets out of reach of English judges, they will find it more difficult to seize your children.**

THE SOONER THE BETTER

- **The sooner you make your plans, the more effective your defences will be. If you have a bank where you are known, or an accountant, or other adviser, tell them that you are planning your long-term security and want their advice.**

- **An offshore trust, or similar protection, is the most effective lasting security against the seizure of your assets by English courts.**

- You should consider this for yourself and also for any sons you have (and perhaps daughters). All young men should have an offshore trust set up at the beginning of their career.

- They should put all their property in the name of the trust. Property in this country should also be kept fully mortgaged. All money, pensions and any other valuable assets should be kept abroad in the trust.

- **Offshore trusts have been used by the wealthy to protect their assets for centuries. Trusts will now become as common as high street bank accounts. The Internet will make this easy.**

- **Keeping unmortgaged assets in the jurisdiction in which you live will come to be seen as a serious mistake. Both divorce courts and tax collectors are waiting to rob you.**

- **See "A Secure Future" .**

BEFORE THE DIVORCE

- **If you have married and now face divorce, consider if these tactics will help you :**

  i) **Bankruptcy**
  If you are close to bankruptcy, or may be in the future, consult your solicitor about whether to apply for bankruptcy before or after divorce, and how this will affect a divorce settlement, maintenance and taxation.

  ii) **Liquid Assets**
  Spend money or other modest assets (like shares).
  See "Finance" .

  iii) **Spend on Credit**
  If you spend on credit cards, make sure that you have a valid reason, for example: you can say it was spent on the family, the home or the children. You will want half this debt deducted from anything your wife gets.

iv) **Cancel Joint Accounts and Her Credit Cards**

Empty and close any joint accounts (or cards) that your wife could use for unjustified expenditure of your money. Keep a record of all money you do give her (and pay her by cheque), so you have evidence of all payments to her.

v) **Pay Cash**

Use cash for any expenditure that you do not want scrutinized and, if necessary, have an explanation ready for withdrawing the cash from an account. Your wife's solicitor will get a judge to order that you give her copies of all statements of all your accounts for at least the last 12 months.

vi) **Keep Complete Financial Records**

Ensure your financial records are as complete as possible. You cannot predict what you will have to prove, or disprove, in a divorce. The better your records, the easier it is for you to avoid any claims that you have hidden assets. Keep your records in a safe place away from home.

vii) **Unemployment for You**

If you become unemployed yourself, then you cannot pay maintenance. There may well be genuine reasons that you cannot work. There may also be reasons that you cannot expect to find work again in the foreseeable future: your age, the nature of your last job, or your skills are out of date.

Judges like you to say that you are keen to work and are trying to find a job. If you think that a judge is trying to give your wife more of your assets because you cannot pay maintenance, say that you will take immediate action in the European Court of Human Rights. Say that you will ask that the judge is required to appear in the ECHR, in Strasbourg, to justify his abuse of your right to own property.

viii) **Employment for Your Wife**

Encourage your wife to work full-time. If she can provide for herself, she does not need maintenance from you. Two households in the future will need two incomes.

ix) **Value Your Assets Conservatively**

You can put a modest value on assets that you intend to keep after divorce, but enhance the value of what she will get. Then you may keep more. A written valuation from a sympathetic "expert" may be helpful.

x) **Gather Information**
Tape record useful conversations or wild outbursts.
See "Negotiation - Information Gathering ".

xi) **A Diary of Marital Faults**
Keep a written record of her affairs, violence, profligate spending and other bad behaviour. Then you can prove that her bad behaviour has been both **"obvious and gross"** and a judge must reduce what assets she is given.

xii) **A Diary of Contact with Your Children**
Keep a written record of everything that you do with your children. Even if this is only for a month or two, it is valuable evidence of how they depend on you every day, to get custody after the divorce. You can send it to the judge before a child residence hearing.

- **Consult your solicitor about which of these tactics you should use and any others he knows of.**

FURTIVE MEASURES

- Some men try to protect themselves from robbers in the divorce courts by concealing assets. They use bank accounts abroad or in someone else's name, or other means. Expect the judge's disapproval if you are caught doing this.

- Beware of concealing any assets for which your wife's solicitor may find documentary evidence. There may be "a paper trail" she can follow if money has ever been in your bank account or has been recorded elsewhere.

- Consult your solicitor, as soon as possible, about what documents you will be forced to give your wife's solicitor.

A SECURE FUTURE

PROTECT IT OR LOSE IT

- **You live in a country in which nothing is safe. The property and the children of honest men are taken every day by unjust courts.** These courts have no interest in the rights of men to their property or the right of children to a stable family and home.

- **It is possible to protect your property from being seized and, if you can do this, it is more difficult for them to take your children.**

- In civilized countries, wealth stays with those who generate it. The property that a man has honestly got is protected for him by the State. This is a fundamental right. But in our country you have lost that protection.

- Here, the State and its courts are now the greatest threat to your possessions. You must therefore arrange your property and money so that they are safe from seizure by English judges.

BANKERS NOT JUDGES

- **Most Englishmen work all their lives to provide a home for their families. They put their trust in English judges to protect their possessions. These Englishmen have mistrusted foreign bankers.**

- **A painful lesson has shown that this was the wrong way round.** Men should have trusted foreign bankers to look after their money. The English judges turned out to be worthless protectors and themselves a threat.

- Theft, by divorce, of the property of honest men in unjust courts now happens on a vast scale. Large numbers of blameless men have walked away from these courts stripped of all their property. Old age pensions are now also stolen.

- **Future generations of Englishmen will never trust an English judge. They will use the services of foreign bankers to lawfully protect their property against judges.**

- Wealthy men have done this for centuries and now so will ordinary men.

HOW TO PROTECT WHAT IS YOURS

- **One of the most effective ways to protect your assets is to put them into a "trust" in another country where property is not seized by courts as it is here. This is called an "offshore trust".**

- A **"trust"** is a legal entity, like a company. If you set one up to protect your assets, you are called the **"settlor"**. This means that you permanently transfer ownership of assets from yourself to the trust.

- A trust is run by a **"trustee"** who lives in that country where the trust is set up. The trustee is often a banker and looks after the assets owned by the trust. The assets can include buildings or land, investments, money and anything else valuable.

- In return for a fee, the trustee will provide regular income or other benefits to any **"beneficiary"** whom the settlor has suggested.

- **The great advantage of this is that the trustee will lawfully refuse to give any of the trust's assets to a divorce court or to tax collectors or creditors.**

- **No court can penalize you because the trustee of your offshore trust will not do what it wants. Assets are therefore protected.**

- In the future, trusts and similar defences will become as common as high street bank accounts.

SETTING UP A TRUST

- A trust is created by a **"deed"**. This document is prepared by a professional adviser and it states what the trust is for and what the trustee will do.

- The kind of offshore trust that you should consider is called a **"discretionary trust"**. This means that the trustee has complete discretion to decide how to use the assets and income of the trust.

- **Create your trust before any threat to your assets arises.**

148

- It is important that you can show that you have <u>permanently and irrevocably</u> given up all control of the assets that you have put into the trust.

- **You cannot therefore comply with any court order to bring the assets back so that they can be seized and given to your wife (or anyone else).**

- To ensure that the trustee understands why you set up the discretionary trust, you will write a **"Letter of Wishes"**. This states the reason for the trust and what you would like him to do with the assets and income.

- You can update the letter whenever you want to. It should say how you would like the trustee to use the assets after you are dead.

- Your Letter of Wishes can only offer the trustee advice and say what you wish him to do. You must not instruct him. He has full control of the trust's assets.

- Your adviser will suggest in which country you should set up your trust. He will have the contacts and experience to do this. You should also seek advice on tax from an accountant recommended by your adviser.

HOW A DISCRETIONARY TRUST WORKS

- **An offshore trust will protect assets against a wife's demands in an English divorce court. There may also be tax benefits.**

- If your trust is set up in a country where there is no income tax, capital gains tax, stamp duty or inheritance tax, then its investments can grow faster and bigger than if it were often robbed by tax collectors.

- If you live in the United Kingdom, then you may have to pay tax when the trustee sends you money. But some people regularly go to live abroad for a time, take a large tax free lump sum while they are there and return to live on it.

- There are other ways of lawfully avoiding tax. Your trustee may decide that the trust should set up a **company (or corporation)**. You may then obtain loans from this company. This allows you to receive money without being liable for tax on it.

- You should discuss with your trustee how this may be done without making yourself vulnerable to demands from a wife who is divorcing you.

- **The combination of an irrevocable, offshore, discretionary trust and a company (or corporation) gives strong, lawful protection against the theft of assets by divorce courts, tax collectors and vexatious creditors.**

- As further protection, you should ask your trustee to take out a 100% mortgage on any property that the trust will hold in the United Kingdom. The money raised should be invested abroad.

- The mortgage should be increased regularly as the value of the property rises. Anything left out of the trust may be seized by an English court.

HOW MUCH YOU SHOULD PAY FOR A TRUST

- **The cost of setting up a standard trust is about £1,500. It can be much more if you want a trust specially created for you.**

- There will be smaller annual charges.

- How much it is worth for you to pay for a trust will depend on the value of the assets that you want the trust to protect. You should also think about any assets that you may get in the future.

EXAMPLES OF TRUSTS

Offshore trusts are located in many financial centres around the World.

Here are examples :

- **Swiss Trusts**

  Switzerland is the largest, low tax centre for private banking in the World. More than a third of all private wealth is protected there. It is a country that has proved a safe and reliable place for foreigners to keep assets for generations.

  Switzerland has secrecy laws to prevent any bank disclosing clients' private affairs to foreign courts and tax collectors. Swiss financial institutions are held in the highest regard for their expertise, probity and discretion.

Swiss banks have, in the past, had a reputation for sometimes being bureaucratic or slow. But this may now be changing. Also, setting up a trust there may be more expensive than in other countries, perhaps 10% more. But Switzerland's virtues outweigh its drawbacks.

- **Bermudian Trusts**

  Bermudian law on trusts is similar to English law and trusts can be created for a period of up to 100 years.

  There must be at least one trustee resident in Bermuda.

  English court judgements and forced inheritance are not recognized in Bermuda.

- **British Virgin Islands Trusts**

  BVI trust law is based on English trust law.

  Trusts can be created for up to 100 years, with modern "wait and see" provisions for what will happen to the trust's assets after that.

  These trusts are usually exempt from all local taxes.

  To protect confidentiality, trusts are exempt from the need to file annual returns and other reporting.

  It is possible to appoint a **"protector of trust"** to oversee and supervise the trustee.

- **St. Vincent and the Grenadines Trusts**

  Trust deeds are held in a confidential government Trust Registry and a certificate issued to the settlor who set up the trust.

  Trust assets are protected against divorce claims and forced inheritance from other jurisdictions, like the United Kingdom.

  Any creditor making a claim against a trust must prove that the settlor created the trust to defraud him and the transfer of assets to the trust left the settlor insolvent.

- **St. Kitts and Nevis Trusts**

    Trust legislation contains modern asset protection provisions.

    Both the trustee and settlor can be beneficiaries of the trust.

    Trusts acting entirely for non-residents are exempt from income, withholding, capital gains and stamp taxes.

    There must be at least 2 trustees and they must have a local office.

    There are strict confidentiality rules for trustees and trusts do not have to be audited.

    The assets of trusts are protected against divorce suits, creditors' claims and forced inheritance.

- **Belize Trusts**

    Belizean trusts have a reputation for modern and flexible asset protection.

    A trust may be created by a written document, or oral declaration, or any other manner.

    Trusts may be registered in a confidential Register but, to protect privacy, this is optional.

    Trusts may be created for up to 120 years and trust income and assets may accumulate for any period within this limit.

PROFESSIONAL ADVICE

- **The law on offshore trusts is complicated and you should get professional advice from a banker or other specialist.**

    You should ask about :

    i)   Which country the trust should be in.

    ii) The cost of setting it up and annual fees and charges.

iii) **The benefits (and any disadvantages) of the trust.**

iv) **How to minimize taxation in this country and where your trust is located.**

v) **What HM Revenue & Customs should be told.**

vi) **<u>Any different offshore solutions for protecting your assets (other than a trust) that your adviser can suggest.</u>**

EXAMPLES OF OTHER OFFSHORE SOLUTIONS

- A trust is one of several ways of protecting your assets. There are other entities that can be used, either by themselves, or combined.

- It is important that any entity that you set up to protect your assets is located offshore, in another jurisdiction, where English courts have no authority.

- Some of these entities allow you to protect what you own without giving away your assets to a trustee, as a trust requires.

Here are examples :

- **Swiss Stock Corporation**

   A Stock Corporation (or "Societe Anonyme" or "Aktiengesellschaft") is a popular Swiss form of company widely used by foreign investors to hold assets.

   A Stock Corporation has its constitution laid down in a document called "articles of association". Accounts must be filed once a year, but these can be abbreviated.

   Capital of 50,000 Swiss Francs must be shown when a Stock Corporation is set up. Directors must be appointed and some of these must be Swiss nationals (often from the bank setting it up).

- **Swiss Holding Company**

   A Holding Company is a Stock Corporation that qualifies for reduced rates of corporate income tax, capital gains tax and net worth tax.

A company is a Holding Company if it holds either a minimum of 20% of the share capital of another corporate entity or holds shares in it worth SFr 2m or more.

- **Swiss Domiciliary Company**

A Domiciliary Company is a Stock Corporation that is foreign-controlled and managed from abroad, with an office in Switzerland (usually at a lawyer's office). The company has no physical presence in Switzerland, conducts most of its business abroad and receives only income from foreign sources.

- **Swiss Auxiliary Company**

An Auxiliary Company is a Domiciliary Company that may conduct a part of its business in Switzerland. Most income must be from a foreign source.

- **Liechtenstein Foundation**

A Liechtenstein foundation (or stiftung) is a legal entity (like a trust) set up by **"a founder"**, to protect personal or family assets. The minimum assets of a foundation are SFr 30,000.

A foundation has **"beneficiaries"** and the founder may have the right to terminate the foundation.

A **"Foundation Deed"** and **"Articles of Association"**, prepared by the founder's adviser, are lodged with the authorities. To preserve confidentiality, these contain only general statements.

A foundation is administered by a board of trustees.

- **Liechtenstein Establishment**

A Liechtenstein establishment (or anstalt) is a corporate entity set up by **"a founder"** and can be used as a holding company for personal assets, patents or royalties. The minimum capital is SFr 30,000.

An establishment has **"beneficiaries"** and the founder's rights can be transferred to others.

If an establishment conducts business, other than the management of investments or other assets, audited annual accounts must be filed.

An establishment is managed by a minimum of one director.

- **Panamanian Foundation**

  A Panamanian foundation is established by **"a founder"** and has **"beneficiaries"**. It is an autonomous legal entity, with no members or shareholders, and can be used for the protection of assets. Minimum capital is US$ 10,000.

  A **"notarized private foundation charter"** is deposited at the Public Registry. Confidential details can be put into separate **"Regulations"** that can be kept private. No accounts or audit are required.

  Panamanian law protects the assets of a foundation against foreign court judgements and forced inheritance.

- **Panamanian Corporation**

  A Panamanian corporation is limited by shares held by at least one shareholder. There is no minimum capital and shares can be either registered or bearer.

  A corporation is formed by at least two **"subscribers"** (or their local nominees) who execute **"Articles of Incorporation"** before a notary and record them at the Public Registry Office.

  A corporation must have a local **"registered agent"** (a lawyer). He holds any bearer share certificate in safe custody and must inform the Registrar about such shares.

  The Articles must name at least three directors.

- **Belize International Business Company**

  A Belize IBC is formed with shares, which may be bearer shares, and must have at least one director. There is no minimum capital, but costs in the first year may be US$ 2,500, and $ 1,000 in subsequent years.

  "Articles and Memorandum of Association" must be filed at the modern, computerized Registry, and an IBC may be incorporated within one hour.

An IBC must have a local **"Registered Agent"** with an office, and no other information is made public about it.

An IBC may hold assets outside Belize and trade in foreign securities, and collect commissions, royalties or dividends.

A trust set up in Belize may incorporate an IBC to hold assets, as extra protection against foreign courts.

- **Nevis Limited Liability Company**

A Nevis LLC is owned by one or more **"members"** who may be individuals or business entities of any nationality. There are no reporting requirements.

There is no Nevis corporation tax, income tax, withholding tax, stamp tax, asset tax or other taxes on assets or income from outside Nevis.

A Nevis LLC may be formed within 2 to 4 working days.

EXPERT, HONEST AND ETHICAL

- **You should ensure that your professional adviser is expert and experienced in offshore business. Your bank may have its own specialist in this, or be able to recommend a suitable firm.**

- Be sure that your adviser understands that you want protection against divorce courts and not just tax advantages.

- Do not invest in anything that you do not understand.

- **All the jurisdictions given above are respectable and none of the solutions here is intended to protect the proceeds of crime.**

USEFUL CONTACTS

- Much preliminary information can be found on the Internet.

- Useful contacts for advice on trusts etc are :

Mr S R Sheikh
GSC Solicitors
31-32 Ely Place
London EC1N 6TD
+44 (0)20 7822 2222
srsheikh@gscsolicitors.com

Red Sea Management, Ltd
Apdo 10455-1000
San Jose, Costa Rica
+506-258-6464
www.redseamanagement.com
info@redseamanagement.com
N. American Toll Free 800-315-4269

MATRIMONIAL CAUSES ACT 1973

THE ACT

- **The Matrimonial Causes Act is the main Act that covers divorce, seizure of assets and similar matters. It slithered onto the statute book in 1973.**

- See the following pages for an extract of some of the main parts of the Act, which may apply to you.

- The extract includes sections 1, 2, 6, 22, 23, 24 and 25 of the Act. These have references to other sections and, if you want to see those, you should buy a full copy of the Act.

- **Your solicitor will tell you about any other laws that apply to you.**

DIFFICULT TO READ

- **The Act is written in difficult and obscure legal English. You do not need to go through this. Parts of it are almost unreadable. Your solicitor will tell you what it means and how it applies to you.**

- The extract is included in this book so that you can see what is being used against you.

IF YOU DO LOOK AT THE ACT

- If you do look at it, you will see that section 1 gives the grounds on which Parliament intended that a divorce could be granted.

- Parliament did not intend that there should be divorce on demand, or that a man's property and children should be seized at his wife's demand. Scandalously, this is what the lawless divorce courts try to impose.

A FULL COPY

- If you want a full copy of the Act, you can buy a paper copy from your nearest Office of Public Sector Information bookshop for £8.40.

- This Act is <u>not</u> shown on the OPSI (HMSO) website: **www.opsi.gov.uk** because only Acts made since 1988 are on the site.

MATRIMONIAL CAUSES ACT 1973

Extract

Divorce on breakdown of marriage

1. – (1) Subject to section 3 below, a petition for divorce may be presented to the court by either party to a marriage on the ground that the marriage has broken down irretrievably.

(2) The court hearing a petition for divorce shall not hold the marriage to have broken down irretrievably unless the petitioner satisfies the court of one or more of the following facts, that is to say –

  (a) that the respondent has committed adultery and the petitioner finds it intolerable to live with the respondent;

  (b) that the respondent has behaved in such a way that the petitioner cannot reasonably be expected to live with the respondent;

  (c) that the respondent has deserted the petitioner for a continuous period of at least two years immediately preceding the presentation of the petition;

  (d) that the parties to the marriage have lived apart for a continuous period of at least two years immediately preceding the presentation of the petition (hereafter in this Act referred to as "two years' separation") and the respondent consents to a decree being granted;

  (e) that the parties to the marriage have lived apart for a continuous period of at least five years immediately preceding the presentation of the petition (hereafter in this Act referred to as "five years' separation").

(3) On a petition for divorce it shall be the duty of the court to inquire, so far as it reasonably can, into the facts alleged by the petitioner and into any facts alleged by the respondent.

(4) If the court is satisfied on the evidence of any such fact as is mentioned in subsection (2) above, then, unless it is satisfied on all the evidence that the marriage has not broken down irretrievably, it shall, subject to sections 3(3) and 5 below, grant a decree of divorce.

(5) Every decree of divorce shall in the first instance be a decree nisi and shall not be made absolute before the expiration of six months from its grant unless the High Court by general order from time to time fixes a shorter period, or unless in any particular case the court in which the proceedings are for the time being pending from time to time by special order fixes a shorter period than the period otherwise applicable for the time being by virtue of this subsection.

Supplemental provisions as to facts raising presumption of breakdown

2. – (1) One party to a marriage shall not be entitled to rely for the purposes of section 1(2)(a) above on adultery committed by the other if, after it became known to him that the other had committed that adultery, the parties had lived with each other for a period exceeding, or periods together exceeding, six months.

(2) Where the parties to a marriage have lived with each other after it became known to one party that the other had committed adultery, but subsection (1) does not apply, in any proceedings for divorce in which the petitioner relies on that adultery the fact that the parties have lived with each other after that time shall be disregarded in determining for the purposes of section 1(2)(a) above whether the petitioner finds it intolerable to live with the respondent.

(3) Where in any proceedings for divorce the petitioner alleges that the respondent has behaved in such a way that the petitioner cannot reasonably be expected to live with him, but the parties to the marriage have lived with each other for a period or periods after the date of the occurrence of the final incident relied on by the petitioner and held by the court to support his allegation, that fact shall be disregarded in determining for the purposes of section 1(2)(b) above whether the petitioner cannot reasonably be expected to live with the respondent if the length of that period or of those periods together was six months or less.

(4) For the purpose of section1(2)(c) above the court may treat a period of desertion as having continued at a time when the deserting party was incapable of continuing the necessary intention if the evidence before the court is such that, had that party not been so incapable, the court would have inferred that his desertion continued at that time.

(5) In considering for the purposes of section 1(2) above whether the period for which the respondent has deserted the petitioner or the period for which the parties to a marriage have lived apart has been continuous, no account shall be taken of any one period (not exceeding six months) or of any two or more periods (not exceeding six months in all) during which the parties resumed living with each other, but no period during which the parties lived with each other shall count as part of the period of desertion or of the period for which the parties to the marriage lived apart, as the case may be.

(6) For the purposes of section 1(2)(d) and (e) above and this section a husband and wife shall be treated as living apart unless they are living with each other in the same household, and references in this section to the parties to a marriage living with each other shall be construed as references to their living with each other in the same household.

(7) Provision shall be made by rules of court for the purpose of ensuring that where in pursuance section 1(2)(d) above the petitioner alleges that the respondent consents to a decree being granted the respondent has been given such information as will enable him to understand the consequences to him of his consenting to a decree being granted and the steps which he must take to indicate that he consents to the grant of a decree.

Attempts at reconciliation of parties to marriage

6. – (1) Provision shall be made by rules of court for requiring the solicitor acting for a petitioner for divorce to certify whether he has discussed with the petitioner the possibility of a reconciliation and given him the names and addresses of persons qualified to help effect a reconciliation between parties to a marriage who have become estranged.

(2) If at any stage of proceedings for divorce it appears to the court that there is a reasonable possibility of a reconciliation between the parties to the marriage, the court may adjourn the proceedings for such period as it thinks fit to enable attempts to be made to effect such a reconciliation.

  The power conferred by the foregoing provision is additional to any other power of the court to adjourn proceedings.

Ancillary relief in connection with divorce proceedings, etc.

Maintenance pending suit.

22. On a petition for divorce, nullity of marriage or judicial separation, the court may make an order for maintenance pending suit, that is to say, an order requiring either party to the marriage to make to the other such periodical payments for his or her maintenance and for such term, being a term beginning not earlier than the date of the presentation of the petition and ending with the date of the determination of the suit, as the court thinks reasonable.

Financial provision orders in connection with divorce proceedings, etc.

23. – (1) On granting a decree of divorce, a decree of nullity of marriage or a decree of judicial separation or at any time thereafter (whether, in the case of a decree of divorce or of nullity of marriage, before or after the decree is made absolute), the court may make any one or more of the following orders, that is to say –

  (a) an order that either party to the marriage shall make to the other such periodical payments, for such term, as may be specified in the order;

  (b) an order that either party to the marriage shall secure to the other to the satisfaction of the court such periodical payments, for such term, as may be so specified;

  (c) an order that either party to the marriage shall pay to the other such lump sum or sums as may be so specified;

  (d) an order that a party to the marriage shall make to such person as may be specified in the order for the benefit of a child of the family, or to such a child, such periodical payments, for such term, as may be so specified;

  (e) an order that a party to the marriage shall secure to such person as may be so specified for the benefit of such a child, or to such a child, to the satisfaction of the court, such periodical payments, for such term, as may be so specified;

(f)   an order that a party to the marriage shall pay to such person as may be so specified for the benefit of such a child, or to such a child, such lump sum as may be so specified;

subject, however, in the case of an order under paragraph (d), (e) or (f) above, to the restrictions imposed by section 29(1) and (3) below on the making of financial provision orders in favour of children who have attained the age of eighteen.

(2) – The court may also, subject to those restrictions, make any one or more of the orders mentioned in subsection (1)(d), (e) and (f) above –

(a)   in any procedings for divorce, nullity of marriage or judicial separation, before granting a decree; and

(b)   where any such proceedings are dismissed after the beginning of the trial, either forthwith or within a reasonable period after the dismissal.

(3) Without prejudice to the generality of subsection (1)(c) or (f) above –

(a)   an order under this section that a party to a marriage shall pay a lump sum to the other party may be made for the purpose of enabling that other party to meet any liabilities or expenses reasonably incurred by him or her in maintaining himself or herself or any child of the family before making an application for an order under this section in his or her favour;

(b)   an order under this section for the payment of a lump sum to or for the benefit of a child of the family may be made for the purpose of enabling any liabilities or expenses reasonably incurred by or for the benefit of that child before the making of an application for an order under this section in his favour to be met; and

(c)   an order under this section for the payment of a lump sum may provide for the payment of that sum by instalments of such amount as may be specified in the order and may require the payment of the instalments to be secured to the satisfaction of the court.

(4) The power of the court under subsection (1) or (2)(a) above to make an order in favour of a child of the family shall be exercisable from time to time; and where the court makes an order in favour of a child under subsection (2)(b) above, it may from time to time, subject to the restrictions mentioned in subsection (1) above, make a further order in his favour of any of the kinds mentioned in subsection (1)(d), (e) or (f) above.

(5) Without prejudice to the power to give a direction under section 30 below for the settlement of an instrument by conveyancing counsel, where an order is made under subsection (1)(a), (b) or (c) above on or after granting a decree of divorce or nullity of marriage, neither the order nor any settlement made in pursuance of the order shall take effect unless the decree has been made absolute.

Property adjustment orders in connection with divorce proceedings etc.

24. – (1) On granting a decree of divorce, a decree of nullity of marriage or a decree of judicial separation or at any time thereafter (whether, in the case of a decree of divorce or of nullity of marriage, before or after the decree is made absolute), the court may make any one or more of the following orders, that is to say –

   (a) an order that a party to the marriage shall transfer to the other party, to any child of the family or to such person as may be specified in the order for the benefit of such a child such property as may be so specified, being property to which the first-mentioned party is entitled, either in possession or reversion;

   (b) an order that a settlement of such property as may be so specified, being property to which a party to the marriage is so entitled, be made to the satisfaction of the court for the benefit of the other party to the marriage and of the children of the family or either or any of them;

   (c) an order varying for the benefit of the parties to the marriage and of the children of the family or either or any of them any ante-nuptial or post-nuptial settlement (including such a settlement made by will or codicil) made on the parties to the marriage;

   (d) an order extinguishing or reducing the interest of either of the parties to the marriage under any such settlement;

subject, however, in the case of an order under paragraph (a) above, to the restrictions imposed by section 29(1) and (3) below on the making of orders for the transfer of property in favour of children who have attained the age of eighteen.

(2) The court may make an order under subsection (1)(c) above notwithstanding that there are no children of the family.

(3) Without prejudice to the power to give a direction under section 30 below for the settlement of an instrument by conveyancing counsel, where an order is made under this section on or after granting a decree of divorce or nullity of marriage, neither the order nor any settlement made in pursuance of the order shall take effect unless the decree has been made absolute.

Matters to which court is to have regard in deciding how to exercise its powers under sections 23 and 24.

25. – (1) It shall be the duty of the court in deciding whether to exercise its powers under section 23(1)(a), (b) or (c) or 24 above in relation to a party to the marriage and, if so, in what manner, to have regard to all the circumstances of the case including the following matters, that is to say –

   (a) the income, earning capacity, property and other financial resources which each of the parties to the marriage has or is likely to have in the foreseeable future;

   (b) the financial needs, obligations and responsibilities which each of the parties to the marriage has or is likely to have in the foreseeable future;

(c) the standard of living enjoyed by the family before the breakdown of the marriage;

(d) the age of each party to the marriage and the duration of the marriage;

(e) any physical or mental disability of either of the parties to the marriage;

(f) the contributions made by each of the parties to the welfare of the family, including any contribution made by looking after the home or caring for the family;

(g) in the case of proceedings for divorce or nullity of marriage, the value to either of the parties to the marriage of any benefit (for example, a pension) which, by reason of the dissolution or annulment of the marriage, that party will loose the chance of acquiring;

and so to exercise those powers as to place the parties, so far as is practicable and, having regard to their conduct, just to do so, in the financial position in which they would have been if the marriage had not broken down and each had properly discharged his or her financial obligations and responsibilities towards the other.

(2) Without prejudice to subsection (3) below, it shall be the duty of the court in deciding whether to exercise its powers under section 23(1)(d), (e) or (f), (2) or (4) or 24 above in relation to a child of the family and, if so, in what manner, to have regard to all the circumstances of the case including the following matters, that is to say –

(a) the financial needs of the child;

(b) the income, earning capacity (if any), property and other financial resources of the child;

(c) any physical or mental disability of the child;

(d) the standard of living enjoyed by the family before the breakdown of the marriage;

(e) the manner in which he was being and in which the parties to the marriage expected him to be educated or trained;

and so to exercise those powers as to place the child, so far as it is practicable and, having regard to the considerations mentioned in relation to the parties to the marriage in paragraph (a) and (b) of subsection (1) above, just to do so, in the financial position in which the child would have been if the marriage had not broken down and each of those parties had properly discharged his or her financial obligations and responsibilities towards him.

(3) It shall be the duty of the court in deciding whether to exercise its powers under section 23(1)(d), (e) or (f), (2) or (4) or 24 above against a party to a marriage in favour of a child of the family who is not the child of that party and, if so, in what manner, to have regard (among the circumstances of the case) –

(a) to whether that party had assumed any responsibility for the child's maintenance and, if so, to the extent to which, and the basis upon which, that party assumed such responsibility and to the length of time for which that party discharged such responsibility;

(b) to whether in assuming and discharging such responsibility that party did so knowing that the child was not his or her own;

(c) to the liability of any other person to maintain the child.

USEFUL WEBSITES

Here are some websites with information that you may find useful or interesting.

Remember that many websites (and books) on divorce are written by people who earn a living from divorce. Some have an interest in promoting divorce and preserving the present system.

UK OFFICIAL WEBSITES

Organisation	Address	Subject /Content
Court Service	**www.courtservice.gov.uk**	Court addresses, lists of cases, forms, fees, guidance, etc
Legal Services Commission	**www.legalservices.gov.uk**	Advice on funding (legal aid) and calculating eligibility.
	www.justask.org.uk	Advice on a wide range of legal matters.
Office of Public Sector Information (Her Majesty's Stationery Office)	**www.opsi.gov.uk**	Legislation since 1988 you can download free. Advice on other publications.
Department for Constitutional Affairs	**www.dca.gov.uk**	Government department responsible for legal system, judges and courts.
Law Society	**www.lawsoc.org.uk**	Directory of solicitors, complaints against solicitors, also legal matters.
Bar Council	**www.barcouncil.org.uk**	Barristers and complaints against barristers.
Office of the Legal Services Ombudsman	**www.olso.org**	Complaints about how the Law Society and Bar Council deal with complaints about solicitors and barristers.
House of Commons	**www.parliament.uk**	Parliament, directory of MPs and their email addresses.

UK PRIVATE WEBSITES

Organisation	Address	Subject / Content
Civitas	www.civitas.org.uk	"Experiments in Living" research on fatherless families and many other publications.
United Kingdom Men's Movement (UKMM)	www.ukmm.org.uk	The men's rights organisation. Marriage, divorce and children.
The Cheltenham Group	www.c-g.org.uk	Men's rights in the family.
INPOWw	www.ukmm.org.uk/ camp/inpoww.htm	The rights of fathers and children.
Parity	www.parity-uk.org	Equal rights group.
Families Need Fathers	www.fnf.org.uk	Information and support for separated parents.
UK Men and Father's Rights Home Page	www.coeffic.demon.co.uk	The rights of men as parents.
The Human-Rights.org	www.human- rights .demon.co.uk	Human rights.
Justice for Fathers UK	www.justiceinfamilylaw .co.uk	Human rights.
International Men's Network	www.mens-network.org	Legal matters.
The Equal Parenting Council	www.equalparenting.org	Promoting equal parenting after divorce.
Terry & Co UK Solicitors	www.terry.co.uk	Information on divorce from a solicitor.
Red Sea Management, Ltd	www.redseamanagement.com	Offshore financial services.
Blackstone's "Commentaries on the Laws of England"	www.yale.edu/lawweb/ avalon/blackstone/ blacksto.htm	The finest statement of the rights and freedoms of the English people; and their Constitution.

EUROPEAN OFFICIAL WEBSITES

Organisation	Address	Subject / Content
European Commission	www.europa.eu.int/comm www.europa.eu.int/comm/sg/lexcomm	Activities of the Commission. Complaints about abuses of rights in the UK.
European Court of Human Rights	www.echr.coe.int	What this Court does and how to apply to it.
European Court of Justice	www.curia.eu.int	What this Court does and how to apply to it.
CELEX	www.europa.eu.int/celex	Complete database of EU law – it is free.
EUR-Lex	www.europa.eu.int/eur-lex	EU treaties and law – it is free.

ANNEXES

Here are examples of documents that you will find useful.

When you prepare your own, type them if you can, or write them neatly by hand. Use A4 paper.

You can make any document as long or as short as you like : one page, or 10 pages, or more.

ANNEX 1

A DIVORCE PETITION

WHAT IS IT ?

- The divorce Petition is a court document, signed by the Petitioner (your wife), that says she wants your marriage dissolved.

- The Petition names you and your wife and children and says where you live. It says when and where you married and if there are any other court proceedings. It gives your wife's grounds for divorce and says if she wants to seize property, income and other assets from you.

HER GROUNDS FOR DIVORCE

- **The Petition will claim that your marriage has "broken down irretrievably" and that at least one of these 5 facts is true :**

  i) **Adultery** by you (and it is intolerable for her to live with you),

  ii) **Unreasonable behaviour** by you,

  iii) **Desertion** by you for 2 years (without her consent).

  iv) **Separation for 2 years** (and you now agree to a divorce),

  v) **Separation for 5 years** (but you do not agree to a divorce),

- The Petition will give details of what your wife claims you have done to justify her divorce.

- You should send an "Answer" to the Petition. This must get to the court office within 28 days and include the fee of £150. (Check that this is still the amount.)

- See the example of a Petition on the next page.

In the   LONDON FAMILY COURT   ~~County Court~~*

*Delete as

appropriate

In the Divorce Registry*   **No.**   LFC00493/2003

(1)   **On the**   13   **day of**   August   1989   **the Petitioner**

     Mrs Linda Francis Osborne (nee Howard)   **was lawfully married to**

     Mr John Michael Osborne   **hereinafter called the Respondent**

     at   The Church of Saint Aphrodite the Blessed, in the Parish of Edenway, in the County of London.

(2)   **The Petitioner and Respondent last lived together as husband and wife**

     at   Rose Cottage, Honeysuckle Lane, London NW2.

(3)   **The Petitioner is domiciled in England and Wales, and is by occupation**

     a   social worker

     and resides at   Rose Cottage, Honeysuckle Lane, London NW2.

     and the Respondent is by occupation a   engineer

     and resides at   Rose Cottage, Honeysuckle Lane, London NW2.

(4)   **There are no children of the family now living _except_**

     Christopher James Osborne   (DOB 11.03.91)

     Susan Josephine Osborne   (DOB 24.12.93)

(5) No other child, now living, has been born to the Petitioner / Respondent during the marriage (so far as is known to the Petitioner) ~~except~~

(6) There have been no other proceedings in any court in England and Wales or elsewhere with reference to the marriage (or to any child of the family) or between the Petitioner and Respondent with reference to any property of either or both of them ~~except~~

(7) There have been no proceedings in the Child Support Agency with reference to the maintenance of any child of the family ~~except~~

(8) There are no proceedings continuing in any country outside England or Wales which are in respect of the marriage or are capable of affecting its validity or subsistence ~~except~~

(9) ~~(This paragraph to be completed only if the Petition is based on five years' separation.) No agreement or arrangement has been made or is proposed to be made between the parties for the support of the Petitioner / Respondent (and any child of the family) except~~

(10) The said marriage has broken down irretrievably.

(11) The Respondent has behaved unreasonably and the Petitioner finds it intolerable to live with the Respondent.

i) The Respondent has recently been drinking heavily. On 14 June 2003, he returned to the matrimonial home in an intoxicated state. He was abusive to the Petitioner and in the argument that followed struck her on the left arm causing a large bruise.

ii) The Respondent is aggressive and bullying towards the Petitioner even when he is not violent. He has frequently been abusive to her in front of the children and treats her dismissively in the company of friends and relatives.

iii) The Respondent has for many months refused to give the Petitioner adequate money for housekeeping, child care and other essential expenses. This has put an unreasonable financial burden on the Petitioner and she has had to obtain a loan from her parents.

iv) The Respondent has always failed to make any contribution to looking after the children. This has meant that the Petitioner has had to care for them entirely by herself in addition to her full time job. This has caused her great pressure and as a result she has been treated by her doctor for stress.

Prayer

The Petitioner therefore prays

(1) The suit

That the said marriage be dissolved.

(2) Costs

That the Respondent may be ordered to pay the costs of this suit.

(3) Ancillary Relief

That the Petitioner may be granted the following ancillary relief:

a)   an order for maintenance pending suit

a periodical payments order

a secured provision order

a lump sum order

For the children:

b)   a periodical payments order

a secured provision order

a lump sum order

c)   a property adjustment order

Signed   *Linda Osborne*

The names and addresses of the persons to be served with this Petition are:

Respondent: Mr John Osborne, Rose Cottage, Honeysuckle Lane, London NW2.

Co-respondent (adultery cases only):

The Petitioner's address for service is: Smith& Jones, Solicitors, High Street, Brent, London NW2.

Dated this   *13ᵗʰ*   day of   *September 2003*

Address all communications for the court to: The Court Manager, London Family Court.

ANNEX 2

A SHORT "ANSWER" TO A "PETITION"

A SIMPLE STATEMENT

- **Your Answer must say that the grounds for divorce in your wife's Petition are false and you contest the divorce.**

- If you have any doubt that you really can show that her grounds are false, or if you think she has strong evidence, it is best just to say her grounds are false and you contest.

YOU CAN GIVE DETAILS IF YOU WANT TO

- If you are confident that all her grounds are false, you can give a few details why.

- Look at her Petition. It will probably give several grounds for divorcing you. Take each one in turn and say that it is not true.
  (Few statements about anything are completely true.)

- If possible, type your Answer, or write it neatly by hand.

WHAT TO DO NEXT

- Send your Answer (and the £150 fee) to the court office within the 28 day deadline. Send a copy to your solicitor and hers.

- You can then decide whether to continue to contest the divorce. If you have put in an Answer to give you a negotiating position, you can decide how to negotiate. (See "Negotiation".)

- See the example on the next page.

IN THE LONDON FAMILY COURT   No LCC1746/2003

Between   **JANE   SIMPSON**   Petitioner

And   **MICHAEL   SIMPSON**   Respondent

ANSWER TO DIVORCE PETITION

This is my Answer to the Petition for divorce that my wife has made.

The grounds for divorce in the Petition are false and I contest the divorce.

Here are my comments :

1. It is not true that our marriage has irretrievably broken down or that I have behaved unreasonably. I treat my wife very well considering her sometimes difficult personality. She has just decided to desert me and her motive is to get my property.

2. I have never committed adultery with Miss Delia Baker, or anyone else, as my wife claims. I have many close friends of both sexes and my relationship with Miss Baker has always been completely innocent and proper. There has never been any sexual contact between us.

3. I did not desert my wife for several months last year. I had to go away on a business trip, which included a long training course. She knew this, we kept in regular contact and I visited her several times (when she was very affectionate).

4. It is completely false that I am violent to my wife. She admits that she has a bit of a temper and this gets worse for several days each month. Whenever she has a go at me, I defend myself and try to restrain her without any hurt to either of us.

5. It is not the case that I refuse to give my wife any housekeeping money. I was unemployed for several months recently and money has been tight. I still pay most of the bills and give her money when I can.

Signed :   Date :

Michael Simpson

Copied to wife's solicitor.

ANNEX 3

A DETAILED "ANSWER" TO A "PETITION"

A LONGER ANSWER

- You can either make your Answer to your wife's Petition short, like the example in Annex 2, or you can include as many details as you like.

- When you write your Answer, this is a valuable chance to say what you think. You may be more comfortable doing this in writing than when you get to the court. Also, saying things twice is often better than just once.

- A detailed Answer can be very convincing.

WHAT IT SHOULD SAY

- **Your Answer must say that the grounds for divorce in your wife's Petition are false and you contest the divorce.**

- You can write your detailed Answer in 2 parts :

    i) **The background** to the problems that your wife is creating.

    ii) **Your response to each of her grounds for divorce given in her Petition.**

- If possible, type your Answer, or write it neatly by hand.

- Your Answer, and the £150 fee, must get to the court office within the 28 day deadline. Copy it to your solicitor and your wife's solicitor.

- You can write more statements to the court whenever you like.

- See the example on the next page.

Between   **HELEN   JOHNSON**   **Petitioner**

And   **HARRY   JOHNSON**   **Respondent**

ANSWER TO DIVORCE PETITION

1. I was very sorry to read the false allegations that my wife has made about our life together. She suffers from a serious mental illness and her allegations are prompted both by her illness and by a feeling that change of any kind to her life will make her feel better. Her grounds for divorce are false and I am vigorously contesting her Petition.

2. For all the time that I have known my wife, Helen, has suffered from schizophrenia. Since our marriage in 1983, she has physically attacked me many hundreds of times without provocation. I have always dealt with her aggression with restraint and tolerance. Despite this, my wife's violent tempers are always short lived, I still have a great deal of affection for her and our household is usually a happy and contented one.

3. It would be a tragedy if our marriage were dissolved at this stage, while the children are still young and need the security and stability of an intact family. I therefore ask the Court to refuse a divorce for the foreseeable future. This will give time for Helen to recover from her current depression and the children will be older and more resilient.

MY WIFE'S MENTAL ILLNESS

4. Helen's illness goes back at least to the time that I first met her in 1980, when she was 21. She was always hyperactive, dashing from one activity to another, before collapsing exhausted. Helen had a terrible temper, which she said that she inherited from her mother, and frequent tearful episodes. Her fits of aggression usually took the form of punching me with her fists or kicking. On one occasion, as I sat on a sofa, she rushed over in one of her rages and sank her teeth into my left ear, causing it to bleed. She broke the glass in 3 pairs of my spectacles (while I was wearing them) before we married. Nevertheless, we became very fond of each other and married in 1983.

5. After our marriage, Helen's schizophrenia became worse. Her physical attacks on me, although usually lasting only a short time, happened more often. As before, they usually took the form of striking me with her fists or trying to kick me. Her attacks are a spectacular display of aggression: her face full of hate, bared teeth, a wild shout and a sudden rush forward with flying fists and feet. The trigger for this behaviour is always something trivial. The underlying cause is emotions deep in Helen's make-up over which she has limited control. When Helen is agitated, almost anything will trigger an attack on me.

6. My response on most occasions has been to catch hold of Helen by the wrists to stop her punching. She would quickly calm down and life would immediately return to normal.

A typical incident may last only 20 seconds. If an attack was particularly violent, I would sometimes push Helen back against a wall and hold her there. She would soon run out of steam, ask me to release her and would then walk away as if nothing had happened.

7. For most of our marriage, these attacks occurred on average twice a week and have happened many hundreds of times over the years. Despite Helen's intimidating behaviour, I have never thought that I was in danger of serious injury and the worst that I sustained was bruises and scratches. I am larger and stronger than she is and am able to restrain her when necessary. It has meant that I have lived with a high degree of stress.

8. My reaction to this persistent aggression has always been to defend myself with the minimum of force, so that neither Helen nor I suffered injury. In the great majority of these incidents, I succeeded. After such an attack, Helen would often laugh at what had happened and apologize. Our 3 children for the most part are accustomed to their mother's attacks on me and usually take little obvious notice. It is just the way that Mummy behaves. However, Jimmie, the youngest (12 in July) has repeatedly said that he finds his mother's tempers frightening.

9. On one occasion, 10 years ago, I was sitting on a cushion in the sitting room listening to music with one of my sons. Helen rushed into the room in one of her wild rages and began punching me. I fended her off without getting up and she left the room. Within a few seconds she returned and began striking me again, so I got to my feet and pushed her against a wall to restrain her until she calmed down. Unfortunately, as I held onto her, one of her fingers was twisted back and dislocated. This is the only occasion, out of many hundreds, that Helen sustained a serious injury as a result of her attacks on me. She told me recently that her reason for this attack was that she had asked me to wash the car but I had gone into the sitting room instead.

10. On several occasions over the past 10 years, Helen has accused me of having affairs. I believe that she now accepts that this is not true.

HELEN'S PRESENT DEPRESSION

11. In April 2001, the nature of Helen's mental illness changed. Her schizophrenia gave way to depression, which has continued to the present. The onset of this severe depression coincided with tests showing that Helen's blood sugar level had fallen seriously, and this (together with her long term vulnerability to schizophrenia) is the main cause of her present illness. Contributory factors may include an attack of German measles which she had recently and a serious car accident that she was involved in several years ago. While working in a night club, Helen obtained for herself a supply of drugs including Ecstasy, Cannabis and Amphetamines. I cannot say whether this drug abuse (or the sudden withdrawal of it, when she left the night club) contributed to her illness.

12. Since she has suffered from depression, Helen's violent behaviour has almost stopped. She has good days, when she seems quite happy, and bad days, when she collapses into despondency and gloom. In this state, she is unable to do her usual activities such as shopping, housework and looking after the children. I am very concerned that, if our family were to break up, this would result in more serious mental problems for Helen.

13. Looking back over the years that Helen and I have spent together, I should have sought professional help for her a long time ago. When I once went to see her doctor about her, 4 or 5 years ago, the doctor had gone on holiday. It was a mistake that I did not

pursue this, but we are private people and I thought that the support of her family would be the best treatment. It was not until August 2001 that Helen went to see a psychiatrist. Although Helen thinks that she is now improved as a result, this psychiatrist's effect on her has been entirely destructive. I do not believe that the treatment has helped Helen at all and it has been a major factor in prompting her to seek a divorce.

11. Helen told me in October 2001 that her doctor wanted her to go to a rest home for treatment, but she has since said that this was not so. I am firmly convinced that Helen will recover from her current depression, but this will only happen if she remains within our family, with both the children and me to support her.

CONCERN FOR OUR CHILDREN

15. Helen has sometimes said that she wishes that she had never married or had a family but, despite this, she is usually good with the children and clearly loves them. But I am gravely concerned that if her wild rages returned, and I was not there to protect them, then one or more of the children might become the target of her aggression.

13. Helen's mental illness must be deeply upsetting for the children, but they all love her and accept her behaviour as her natural behaviour. Tara (15), though the eldest and most eloquent, is not yet emotionally grown-up. She has an unquestioning loyalty to her mother, while I seldom get a polite word from her. It is difficult for me to decide exactly what she thinks of the exact nature of her mother's illness.

17. Phillip (13) is a quiet boy and has severe attention-deficiency. It is vital that the stable family where he feels secure is kept together. For Phillip a divorce would be traumatic, with long term consequences for his well being and development. He learnt of his mother's intention to seek a divorce in March and said that he does not want it to happen. I have been told by several of his teachers that he is no longer able to concentrate on his work at school and has become disruptive in class. This is very worrying and points to much worse effects if a divorce were granted.

18. Jimmie (12 in December) is slightly dyslexic and is most obviously affected by his mother's emotional behaviour. He says that he thinks her tempers are frightening and is visibly upset by her belligerence. He has said repeatedly that he does not want a divorce. As he is the youngest, I give him most emotional support and he is clearly very attached to me.

FURTHER DIFFICULTIES FOR MY WIFE

19. Since October 2001, Helen has met a psychologist, Jezebel Finklestein, twice a month. Helen's first meeting with this woman caused her great distress, but she since appears to have become dependent on her. Their subsequent meetings have given Helen a powerful conviction that I am to blame for her mental state. This psychologist has also told my wife that she is on the verge of alcoholism because she drinks 2 gin and tonics a day, which is ridiculous.

20. I know of no sound evidence that analysis helps depression, and I am appalled at the effect that it has had on my wife. This psychologist has had a very destructive influence on Helen and I think it is unlikely that we would now be facing divorce without her influence.

I ask that the Court disregard her opinions. The Court might find it helpful to ask for a second medical opinion.

21. Helen has also told me that her lawyers have advised her that this is the most auspicious time for her to seek a divorce, because she could expect to obtain more of my property now. This does not seem responsible advice for lawyers to give someone with children whose judgement is affected by mental illness. I think that it is most unfortunate that my wife has been pushed along by outsiders in this way, when she is so vulnerable.

MY RESPONSE TO THE GROUNDS FOR DIVORCE IN MY WIFE'S PETITION

19. I do not agree with Helen's statement that I have behaved unreasonably and as a result she cannot be expected to live with me. This is the exact opposite of the truth. I have explained above that I have always treated Helen and her illness with as much kindness and understanding as I could. I am saddened that, as a result of her illness, she has forgotten all the help and support that I have shown her over the many years that she has suffered from schizophrenia. Many of the complaints in her Petition are completely false. They are perjury and a deliberate attempt to deceive the Court.

23. **This is my response to her grounds for divorce :**

a) Helen claims that I no longer care for my family.

This is not true. I am at home at least 6 days a week, returning from work via Tescos every night at about 7pm. I often supervise Jimmie while he has a bath and prepares for bed. We all discuss what we have done that day, the children's interests and other family matters. I often cook for Helen and me after she has prepared the children's meal. Last week, I alone cooked a roast joint and everything that goes with it for the family. Every evening we all get together in the sitting room beside the fire and I am always ready to help the children with their homework. Other interests that I share with the children include: reading Tolken's stories, country walks, gardening, fishing, skiing and holidays. I have taken my family to Wales for holidays many times and also to Italy, Spain, Corsica and Belgium. I include Helen and the children in all outside activities.

b) Helen claims that I do not help to look after the children.

This is completely untrue. I take a very close interest in all my children. Phillip suffers from severe attention-deficiency syndrome and I have taken the lead in pursuing Brickley Council and his school to the Educational ADS Board. After a great deal of effort, I was successful in obtaining the special help for Phillip that the Council is required by law to provide but had tried to economize on. I attend the reviews of Phillip's performance at his school, and meet all my children's teachers as often as I can. Only a concerned and active parent would do this.

Last July, I took all the children to Wales to stay in a beach house for 2 weeks. While we were there we went swimming, boating, windsurfing and rock climbing. Evenings in the house included games and other entertainments. This was an exciting, adventure holiday on which I had sole care of my children. Helen refused to come with us even though invited, but encouraged us to go. She clearly would not have done so if she had any real doubts about my competence to look after our children.

My wife's claim that she has had to care for the children on her own for years is silly and completely untrue and is a deliberate fabrication. Helen knows full well that I spend a great deal of time with my family and take a keen interest in their welfare. I do not remember an alleged occasion 4 years ago when she says that I left her to look after that children unaided for more than a week. It does not surprise me that she cannot think of any real examples of neglect more recently.

c) Helen claims that I have been aggressive to her.

This is false. I have already described how I have done my best to cope with my wife's wild rages and depression. I have done so with much kindness and understanding, in very difficult circumstances, over a long time. On the hundreds of occasions when she has physically attacked me I have always responded with restraint. I think that it is ungrateful and disloyal of her that she now thinks it is convenient to falsely claim that I, and not her, am the violent one.

Shortly before the delivery of her divorce Petition, Helen said to me that she thought that I was a "decent man" and a "generous man", which shows her confusion. I have explained already how one of her attacks on me led to an injury to one of her fingers.

I have never pushed Helen over in the garden as she claimed in her Petition. However, over the last 20 years, Helen has attacked me many times in and around the house and, when her attack takes the form of violent pushing, then I stand my ground and push back until she runs out of steam and walks away. Nearly all Helen's attacks on me have been in or around the house and in private.

d) *Helen claims that I do not tell her anything about family finances.*

This is not true. Helen is rather a spendthrift and since we married we have always had separate bank accounts. This has always been to Helen's advantage as it has left her with all the surplus income every month, which she has decided how to spend. Throughout our marriage, Helen has left most financial matters to me. She has always refused to contribute to any of the main household bills or pay for holidays. We discuss money and other plans whenever she decides to show an interest.

Helen has always been extravagant beyond our financial means. As a catering manager, on a modest income, I have nevertheless managed to provide us with a comfortable home with 4 bedrooms, 2 large reception rooms and 2 bathrooms. I have only been able to do this by careful management of money and working overtime when it was available. For the whole of our marriage, all my resources and energy have gone to providing for my family.

e) Helen claims that I do not support my family or contribute financially.

This is completely false. From the beginning of our marriage, I alone have paid every mortgage premium. I have also paid all the monthly household bills, including: electricity, gas, Council Tax, insurance, telephone and water rates. Helen has always refused any contribution to the mortgage or these other monthly bills despite having an income after tax of £1,000-1,200 per month for most of the past 12 years. This has meant that for long periods I have had to cover family expenditure using a bank overdraft. It is therefore my wife who has not made a reasonable contribution to family finances.

Helen's claim that I spend only £30 on food for my family each week is not true. She knows that I make 5 visits to Tescos every week and at present spend about £110 a week there. I am afraid that she is being deliberately deceitful about this.

It is true that in 1995 a small publishing business that I set up made a loss of £9,000. This was an attempt to improve my finances, which was not successful. However, it is a modest amount in comparison with what I have paid into the family budget over 21 years.

f) Helen claims that my behaviour has caused her depression.

This is not true. I have given the history of my wife's mental illness earlier in this statement. She has suffered from schizophrenia for many years and her vulnerability to this illness almost certainly dates from before I first met her. I am concerned that her doctors only seem to recognize Helen's recent depression and have not properly addressed its long term nature. I have always done my best to deal with her fierce tempers and depression sympathetically and I am saddened that she now pretends not to realize this.

CONCLUSION

24. My wife's claim, in her divorce Petition, that my behaviour towards her is unreasonable is vexatious and completely false. Helen has not been well and her judgement has been affected by this. At the same time she is motivated by the large financial reward that she thinks that she will get by divorcing me. She told me that her solicitors have said that she can expect to seize most of the property that I have worked for all my life if she gets rid of me now. Her grounds for divorce are cold-blooded lies to achieve this.

25. I have done nothing to deserve this kind of treatment. My behaviour has always been reasonable, despite the difficulties that I have had to deal with. To take away my children and seize most of my property, because that is what a dishonest woman wants, would be an outrageous injustice. Her ruthlessness is demonstrated by the perjury that she is prepared to commit to get what she wants. I trust that the Court will not grant a divorce on the basis of falsehoods.

26. The children's welfare is very important. Tara will soon be 13, but the boys are still young. Phillip's attention-deficiency is severe, Jimmie's less so, but it is essential for their happiness and proper development that the family where they feel secure is kept together. This should be the main priority.

27. I oppose this divorce. The law does not allow for a divorce in these circumstances and I ask that the Court rejects my wife's Petition. I will also certainly resist a judicial separation if she asks for one.

Signed :   Date :

George Johnson

Copied to wife's solicitor.

ANNEX 4

A SCHEDULE OF ISSUES

A LIST OF WHAT YOU DISAGREE ABOUT

- Before the first court hearing, you will probably be asked to produce a "Schedule of Issues". This is a list of all the things that you and your wife disagree about.

- This can include :

  i) Whether or not she gets her divorce.

  ii) Whether she should get any of your assets or maintenance.

  iii) Where children will live if there is a divorce.

  iv) What her future income is likely to be.

  v) Anything else that you think will affect you (or your children) during the divorce or afterwards.

- If possible, type your Schedule, or write it neatly by hand.

- Send a copy to the court office, your solicitor and your wife's solicitor.

- Your wife will also produce her own Schedule and you will be sent a copy.

- See the example on the next page.

| Between | PAULINE | SQUIRES | Petitioner |
| And | DAVID | SQUIRES | Respondent |

RESPONDENT'S SCHEDULE OF ISSUES

The issues that we disagree about include :

1. This is a contested divorce and I am sure that I can show that the grounds for divorce in my wife's Petition are false. Therefore, a divorce may not happen.

2. If a divorce happens, my wife says that she wants 60% of the equity in our home. This is completely unacceptable. She made only a small contribution to our finances for years and preferred to spend her money on other things. She should get one third of the equity.

3. My wife has not provided herself with a pension and now wants half of mine. She had plenty of opportunity to pay into a pension fund for many years and it is irresponsible that she did not. It is unreasonable that she should now expect to seize any of mine.

4. My wife says that I have not declared all my assets and am hiding things away. This is not true and she has no evidence of it.

5. My wife has understated her earning capacity. She is a fit woman and is perfectly capable of working full time to earn an income similar to mine. Many women in her circumstances now have careers and so should she.

6. My wife says that all the children should live with her after a divorce. I do not agree. The children have often said that they would prefer to live with me and I am just as capable of looking after them. I am very concerned that pressure is being put on them by my wife and Welfare Officers and others to make them say that they want to go with her.

Signed :   Date :

David Squires

Copied to wife's solicitor.

ANNEX 5

A QUESTIONNAIRE

FIND OUT ABOUT YOUR WIFE'S FINANCES

- Soon after you get your wife's divorce Petition, you will have to make a Financial Declaration. (See "What Happens Next" Step 7.) Your wife will also have to make one and you will get a copy.

- You are entitled to write a "Questionnaire" asking your wife to provide you with any further information that you want about her finances or any other matter.

- You can ask about :

    i)   All assets that your wife has now, or has had in the past, or may have in the future, including: property, money, shares, jewellery and personal effects.

    ii) Her pension, how long she has paid into it, its current value and what it will be worth when she is old enough to get income from it.

    iii) Her present income, what she has earned in the past and is capable of earning by full-time work in the future.

    iv) Anything else that you want to know about her finances, or other matters, that you think is relevant to any of the court proceedings.

- Included as many questions as you like and ask for documentary evidence of everything you ask for.

- If possible, type your Questionnaire, or write it neatly by hand.

- See "Finance" .

- See the example on the next page.

Between   **JANICE**   **JACKSON**   **Petitioner**

And   **MARK**   **JACKSON**   **Respondent**

RESPONDENT'S QUESTIONNAIRE

Please would my wife produce :

1. Evidence to support her allegation that I have not made a full disclosure of my finances, including details of the shares that she says that I have not disclosed, the policies that she says I have concealed (other than the two I declared with Abbey National) and details of a second bank account that she says I have, with documentary evidence.

2. Documentary evidence of the annual salary scale that she is on as a part-time Press Officer in Nationwide Electronics PLC and say where she falls on the scale. Also, what she would expect to earn if she were to work full-time and her prospects for overtime and promotion.

3. A realistic estimate of the annual profit that she could expect to make if she restarted the dress making business that she ran in her spare time until 2 years ago. Also, evidence of the income that she got from this business, whether it was declared for tax or not.

4. Documentary evidence of the money and all other things that she inherited when her Uncle George died in 2001. Will she say where the money is now and supply evidence.

5. A list of all payments, of more than £500, in or out of her bank account over the last 12 months. Will she include a statement for each payment of where the money came from or was going to, with documentary evidence.

6. A list of all life assurance, and other policies (and investments) in which she has an interest. This should include all policies which have matured, or been released, in the last 5 years or which will mature in the next 5 years. In each case the policy number should be given and documentary evidence of the value of the policy.

7. Her Lloyds TSB Trustcard statements for the last 2 years.

8. Details of any relative, or trust, who will provide her with property, accommodation, financial support or other benefit in the future. This should include full details of the property that her parents have been promising to give her for several years.

9. Documentary evidence of where her income has gone over the last 2 years. As she has always refused to make any contribution to mortgage premiums or monthly household bills, this should cover more than £1,000 a month that she has had left after buying food, petrol and clothes.

10. An independent expert valuation of her collection of china dolls. This to include a separate valuation of any item worth more than £100.

11. Copies of her tax returns for the last 3 tax years.

12. A statement of why she now demands that all our children should be made to live with her in future, regardless of their wishes. We agreed only a few weeks ago that each of the children was old enough to decide which parent he should live with but she has now changed her mind.

Signed :   Date :

Mark Jackson

Copied to wife's solicitor.

ANNEX 6

A CHILD RESIDENCE STATEMENT

A STATEMENT

- Child residence or "custody" means who your children will live with after divorce or separation.

- **You may be asked by a judge to make a written Child Residence Statement about where your children will live if there is a divorce.** You will be able to say how long you need to write it. Allow yourself several weeks.

- **If you are not asked to produce a Statement, you can still say that you want to write one.** You do not need anyone's permission to do this.

- If possible, type your Statement, or write it neatly by hand.

IT HELPS TO WRITE IT DOWN

- Unless you are a very fluent speaker, it is easier to write down what you want for your children than to say it for the first time when you get to the court. You can send a copy to the court well before the hearing at which the judge is going to decide where your children will live.

- Copy your Statement to your solicitor and your wife's solicitor.

- On your own copy of the Statement, use a high-lighter pen to mark all the main points you want to make at the court hearing. You can then use your written Statement to remind you what to say when you speak to the judge. Ask him to confirm that he has already read your Statement.

- See the example on the next page.

IN THE LONDON FAMILY COURT   **No LFC1939/2003**

Between	**FIONA**	**DICKENS**	**Petitioner**
And	**ROBIN**	**DICKENS**	**Respondent**

RESPONDENT'S STATEMENT ON CHILD RESIDENCE

1. This is a statement of my proposals and concerns about the future of our children should my wife, Fiona, obtain a divorce. I have written this statement on the assumption that the Judge has already read my Answer to my wife's divorce Petition. That document describes in detail my wife's irresponsible behaviour and matters relating to our children's welfare.

2. What I want to say here is that both our children should be allowed to decide for themselves which parent to live with if there is a divorce. If, after the divorce, either of the children finds that he has made a mistake, and wishes to change to the other parent, he should be able to do so without interference. The children's wishes may not be the Court's only consideration, but this should be the main factor.

3. Our 2 children are : Simon 13 and Thomas 11. Both are sufficiently mature to have thought carefully about whom they would want to live with in the future. However, my wife has never been willing to spend as much time with the children as they need, her career and social life have always come first. If either of the boys goes to live with her, it should be under a joint custody order. I will also ask that he be put on the Child Protection Register for close monitoring by the Social Services.

SIMON

4. Simon is now 13 years old. Although an intelligent boy, he has suffered from asthma since he was a baby and will inevitably be badly affected by his mother's plans to break up his family. Nevertheless, he is fully able to make a decision about which of his parents he should live with in future.

5. Simon is very fond of both his parents and he says that he could live with either. If he goes with his mother initially, then it should be under a joint custody order. This would allow him to move to his father if he found life with her was too difficult. I am concerned that the trauma that his mother's divorce proceedings are causing him will make his asthma worse and permanently affect his school work.

THOMAS

6. Thomas is 11 and, although younger than his brother, is in some ways the more mature of the two. His judgement on most things is grown up, he is consistent in his views and can be relied on to give a sensible opinion on most things. On a boating holiday in Cornwall last year, he played a full part as a member of the crew of the fishing smack that we hired.

190

7. Thomas has said repeatedly that he does not like his mother's new boy friend. He first heard of her intention to break up our family in April. Without prompting, he came to me in May and said "If you and Mum get divorced, can I live with you - not just at weekends but all the time?". Since then he has been consistent that he would live with his father and not join his mother's new household.

8. When Thomas went to the London Family Court on 14 July 2003, he and his brother were interviewed by a Welfare Officer in a separate room. Thomas confirmed that he wished to live with me. He considers that he has the right to make this decision for himself and will be very distressed if he is made to live with his mother against his will. I was concerned and angry at the pressure that was put on him by the Welfare Officer to say that he wanted to live with his mother. It would be unreasonable and cruel to force him to live with his mother, and her friend, when he has said repeatedly that he wants to live with me.

9. The only reasonable solution therefore is that Thomas should live with me if there is a divorce. He would be free to see his mother as frequently as he wishes. Should he change his mind about whom he wants to live with, I would not object to an immediate move.

MY CONCERNS ABOUT MY CHILDREN'S FUTURE

10. In my Answer to the divorce Petition, I expressed concerns about our children living with my wife after a divorce. I do not like her new boyfriend and do not think that he is a suitable man to have care of my children. It is significant that it is our younger child who has taken a strong dislike to him and has said repeatedly that he wants to live with his father.

11. Fiona readily admits that she has a fierce temper. She clearly understands at present, that with divorce proceedings, it is strongly in her interest to behave calmly at all times. This constraint will not be there after a divorce. Without my presence to absorb her anger, one or more of the boys might become her target.

12. Despite the present incentive for behaving responsibly, Fiona has shown that she is more interested in her own social life than in the boys' welfare. When I went away on business for 3 nights recently, my sons told me on my return that their mother had stayed out every night until after midnight, leaving them alone. I am afraid that incidents like this will become frequent if my wife gets a divorce.

CONCLUSION

13. I am well able to care for and support my sons financially. I have flexible working hours and am accustomed to looking after them. There is a strong bond between me and my boys. Their aunt (my sister), who lives close by, has also offered to help. I intend to live within reach of their school. (Fiona has given no undertaking about where she will live but has indicated that she is thinking of going back to Derbyshire where she was born. It worries Simon that he may be uprooted from his school where he has only just become settled.)

14. Both boys are able to make a clear judgement about whom they want to live with. They have very different personalities and interests and, although they must have frequent contact, it is not essential that they be constantly together. Simon has not yet made up his

mind who he would prefer to live with, whereas his younger brother is determined to live with me. In any event, either may decide with his feet where to go.

15. The boys have lived with their mother's irresponsible behaviour for many years and it may be in their best interests that they now have more stable surroundings. It is also probably true that the boys have reached an age when they have the greatest need of a father. Should the Court decide that it is in the boys' best interests, I would of course be happy to make a home for both of them.

Signed :   Date :

Robin Dickens

Copied to wife's solicitor.

ANNEX 7

A WITNESS STATEMENT

DO YOU NEED A WITNESS ?

- At most Divorce Court hearings, there are no witnesses. But there may be at a contested divorce hearing or a child residence hearing.

- There are 2 kinds of witness :

  i) An expert witness, such as a "Welfare Officer" or child psychologist, who may say what they think is best for your family.

  ii) An ordinary witness who may be asked to attend by either you or your wife to support what you say. This can be a friend or someone else who knows about your family.

- You can call as many witnesses as you like, or none at all.

- If you want to produce a witness, consult your solicitor and tell your wife's solicitor.

A WITNESS STATEMENT

- If there is plenty of time before a hearing, you can ask your witness to write a Statement to be sent to the court (and your wife's solicitor) before the hearing.

- The Statement should say briefly what evidence the witness wants to give.

- See the example on the next page.

IN THE LONDON FAMILY COURT   No FD1805/2003

Between   ANN   HURLEY   Petitioner

And   CHARLES   HURLEY   Respondent

WITNESS STATEMENT OF KEITH ROBERTS

I, **KEITH MARTIN ROBERTS**, an estate agent, of 23 Harringdon Road, Cropwell, Lancashire. make the following statement knowing its contents to be true and that it will be placed before the court as my evidence.

1. I have been an estate agent for 7 years and before that was a draftsman with a firm of chartered surveyors in Blackwell. I first met the Respondent, Charles Hurley, about 10 years ago when we worked together on a building project for which he was the assistant manager. We have been friends since then. I was best man at his wedding when he married Ann in 1997.

2. I understand that Ann has said that she wishes to divorce Charles because his behaviour is unreasonable and she cannot be expected to live with him. This came as a surprise to me because Charles is one of the most easy going and gentlemanly men I know.

3. I have seen Charles and Ann frequently throughout their marriage and have often been a visitor in their home. On these many occasions Charles's behaviour has always been calm and courteous to everyone present, including Ann. This was in contrast to Ann's behaviour which was sometimes rude and quarrelsome towards her husband. On one occasion I saw her hit him over the head at a party because he had displeased her.

4. Charles has confided in me that Ann is frequently aggressive at home but he deals with her tantrums with restraint and they seldom last long. He is still fond of her and is contesting her divorce Petition because he thinks that it is essential to keep the home together for the sake of their 2 children, John and Sarah.

5. Charles has told me that Ann has said to him quite bluntly that her plans to divorce him are motivated entirely by her wish to sell the house which his parents left him. Her solicitor has told her that she should demand that all the equity be given to her. This would be to house her and the children after she has deserted her husband. In private she has never pretended that she has any genuine complaint about Charles's conduct.

6. I would be very sorry to see Charles and Ann's marriage end. I have no doubt that with good will on both sides, they can have an enjoyable future together and that is, without question, what is best for their children.

7. I would be willing to come to court and answer questions about my evidence.

Dated :

Signed………………………………………….

KEITH MARTIN ROBERTS

ANNEX 8

A DIVORCE SUIT RECORD

CONTESTING HER DIVORCE

- "A divorce suit hearing" is also called "a contested divorce" or "a defended divorce". They all mean the same.

- If you put in an "Answer" to your wife's divorce Petition, you have the option of contesting her divorce at a court hearing. You may be able to prevent her getting a divorce and seizing your property.

- See "What Happens Next - Step 12".

- See "Contesting The Divorce".

A WRITTEN RECORD

- If you do have a contested divorce hearing, you should make written notes of everything important said in court, especially the Judge's decision at the end. Take lots of paper with you. You will need your notes when you consult your solicitor later.

- After the hearing, you should use your rough notes to write out a clear statement of the Judge's decision and his reasons. This will be your only detailed record of what has been done to you.

- If you intend to appeal against the result of the hearing, you should write a detailed statement of everything important that happened at the hearing. You will also need this if you intend to complain to the European Courts about the abuse of your rights.

- This statement will be important evidence of a wrong decision by the Judge, or the abuse of your rights.

- See the example of a detailed statement on the next page.

IN THE PRINCIPAL REGISTRY OF THE FAMILY DIVISION   FD04D01854

Between	**ANDREA**	**BROWNE**	**Petitioner**
And	**IAN**	**BROWNE**	**Respondent**

DIVORCE SUIT HEARING

IN FRONT OF JUDGE UPWRIGHT

RECTITUDE HOUSE, LONDON ON 8 DECEMBER 2004

1. **Judge Upwright** said that he noted that the Petitioner, Mrs Browne, was represented in the proceedings by her barrister, Mr Craven, while the Respondent, Mr Browne, represented himself.

2. It was a part of a judge's task to ensure that any "litigant in person", representing himself, was kept fully informed of what was happening, and this he would do. Mr Browne was free to ask him a question whenever there was anything that he did not understand.

3. **Judge Upwright** said that the bundle of papers relating to the case, prepared by Mrs Browne's solicitor, was very helpful, and it included documents that Mr Browne had provided as evidence for this hearing. He saw that Mr Browne had a copy of the bundle.

4. **Judge Upwright** said that he would be grateful if Mr Craven would begin by explaining the circumstances of the case.

WIFE'S BARRISTER'S INTRODUCTION

5. **Mr Craven** said that the marriage had been celebrated on 7 June 1991 and there were two children, Stephen (12) and Lisa (10).

6. The family continued to live in the matrimonial home, but Mrs Browne had moved into a separate bedroom nearly 12 months ago. Mr Browne continued to share mealtimes with the children, though Mrs Browne usually ate separately.

7. Mrs Browne had signed her divorce Petition on 26 November 2003 and it had been sent to Mr Browne on 3 January 2004. Her grounds for divorce were that the marriage had broken down irretrievably, and there had been unreasonable behaviour by Mr Browne, such that she could not reasonably be expected to live with him.

8. Mrs Browne's Petition gave the following evidence of Mr Browne's unreasonable behaviour:

i) Mr Browne had often been aggressive and abusive to Mrs Browne, which she found very upsetting.

ii) There were clear indications that Mr Browne had had sexual relations with at least one other woman when he was away from home, ostensibly on business. Mrs Browne was a woman of strong religious convictions. She believed in marital fidelity and found Mr Browne's unfaithfulness unacceptable.

iii) Mr Browne had shown little interest in the children when they were small and had never properly supported and contributed to the family financially. Mrs Browne had for many years been obliged to pay for all the children's needs.

9. Mr Browne had submitted an Answer to the Petition on 21 January 2004. Neither party had brought any witnesses to this hearing.

HUSBAND'S INTRODUCTION

10. **Judge Upwright** asked Mr Browne to give a brief response to the main points that had been made.

11. **Mr Browne** said that his wife's divorce Petition was all false. She had committed perjury, with the intention of stealing his property and separating him from his children. Nothing that she said could be trusted, and she should not benefit in any way from this deception.

12. The Common Law guaranteed his right to own and enjoy his own property, to family life, and to bring up his children. These ancient rights were confirmed by the European Convention on Human Rights. It was disgraceful that fundamental rights could be dishonestly challenged in this way.

13. He had always treated his wife well, with consideration and restraint, even in difficult circumstances. The damage that divorce did to children was well known and he did not want his children to suffer it because of his wife's false accusations and selfish demands.

WIFE ANSWERS HER BARRISTER'S QUESTIONS

14. **Mrs Browne** entered the Witness Box and took the oath.

15. **Mr Craven** then questioned her about the documents she had submitted, her marriage, and her reasons for seeking a divorce.

16. **Mrs Browne** confirmed that the divorce Petition was hers and that the signature on other documents she had submitted was hers.

17. She said that her husband was always nice to her in other people's company but he was intimidating in private. On several occasions he had stood very close to her and clenched

his fists. He sometimes called her names and once banged his hand hard against a wall. The children were always very upset by this conflict between their parents.

18. **Mrs Browne** said that she was sure that her husband had been committing adultery with other women, for many years, when he travelled away from home for his work. He once hung his jacket on a chair and, when it fell off, a packet of coloured condoms fell out. He had never used coloured condoms with her. She had seen the packet before and the number of condoms in it went down regularly.

19. She had always known that her husband had an eye for the ladies, even before they married. It was deeply upsetting to her as she came from a religious background and believed in loyalty and faithfulness in marriage.

20. **Mrs Browne** said that her husband had always been tight with money. She had always had to pay for her own car and provide the children with much of their clothing, entertainment, school trips and other needs. She also had to contribute to the weekly budget for food and general household expenses, because her husband did not give her enough housekeeping.

21. Her husband had a passion for golf and this was where most of his surplus income went. It had always meant that Mrs Browne had not only to spend nearly half her own salary on essential items, but also taken most of the responsibility for caring for the children.

22. **Mr Craven** thanked Mrs Browne for her answers.

WIFE ANSWERS HUSBAND'S QUESTIONS

23. **Judge Upwright** said that Mr Browne could now put any questions he wished to Mrs Browne.

24. **Mr Browne** asked his wife to agree that her story that he intimidated her in private was not true. He was not in the habit of clenching his fists or being deliberately offensive, was he?

25. **Mrs Browne** replied that she stood by her statements about that. They both knew how he behaved and she had decided that the relationship was over. It was all his fault.

26. **Mr Browne** asked whether it was she who put the coloured condoms that she claimed to have found in his jacket pocket. Had she any true evidence of any kind that he had ever had sex with another woman during their marriage?

27. **Mrs Browne** said that it was ridiculous to suggest that she would put condoms in his pocket. He was very good at covering his tracks, but there were many unexplained absences at weekends. Golf could be a convenient excuse for all sorts of things.

28. **Mr Browne** said that he suspected that it was in fact Mrs Browne who had been involved in an extra-marital relationship. Was this true?

29. **Mrs Browne** said that it was not.

30. **Mr Browne** said that, in her divorce Petition, Mrs Browne had said that he had not supported and contributed to the family financially. Would she say who had provided a family home since 1991, who had paid all the mortgage premiums and all the other monthly household bills, including: gas, electricity, council tax, water rates, insurance and telephone?

31. **Mrs Browne** said that he had. That was what men were expected to do. She had meant that she had to pay many of the children's day to day expenses. He never gave her enough housekeeping and she was forced to use some of her own income for things that he should be paying for.

32. **Mr Browne** said that he was surprised that in Mrs Browne's Petition she claimed that he had showed little interest in the children. She knew that he loved them and spent as much time as he could with them. Why had she made this false claim?

33. **Mrs Browne** replied that she knew very well that he was fond of the children. But there had been many times in the past when she needed help and, for one reason or another, he was not available to give it. Other men did more with their children than he did.

HUSBAND GIVES HIS EVIDENCE

34. **Judge Upright** asked Mr Browne to go into the witness box and take the oath. Mr Browne could say what he wanted to about his wife's demand for a divorce. He would then be questioned by Mrs Browne's barrister.

35. **Mr Browne** said that he had been horrified to receive a divorce Petition and by many of the things said about him in it. It simply was not true that the marriage had broken down irretrievably. Family life continued more or less as it always had. Mrs Browne did often join him and the children for meals, whatever her barrister said. They all still went for walks together occasionally, though the children were less interested in this now that they were older.

36. He and his wife had gone on a week's holiday together in the Summer. It had been to the Bahamas, which is a romantic location and they had a wonderful time. He had thought afterwards that their marriage was back on a firm footing and that his wife would withdraw her Petition. He now realised that she had an ulterior motive for continuing with the divorce.

37. The coloured condoms that Mrs Browne claimed to have found in his jacket pocket were a complete mystery to him. He had only ever bought the vanilla variety, which he and Mrs Browne had always found perfectly satisfactory. He strongly suspected that the coloured condoms had been put in his jacket by Mrs Browne, as evidence for her divorce. The only other explanation was that they were a practical joke by friends at the golf club, but this was unlikely.

38. Mrs Browne's allegations that he was aggressive and abusive were simply not true. When there was any conflict or disagreement, it was usually she who started it, and he tried to respond sensibly and calm her down. His wife was trying to give a false picture of both their relationship and family life. Their home was usually happy and normal.

39. **Mr Browne** said that he had included many bank statements, and other papers, in the bundle of papers his wife's solicitor had prepared for the hearing. These showed beyond any doubt that his wife's allegation that he did not support his family was untrue. He was the main breadwinner and always had been. He paid all the main bills and his wife's contribution on essential items was quite small.

40. Last year, Mr Browne had received a modest inheritance. His mother had died and left him a small house. Rising house prices meant that, for the first time, he had a substantial amount of money. There was no doubt that this was a major incentive for his wife to divorce him. It was disgraceful that we had courts in this country where an unscrupulous woman could expect to steal from her husband.

41. **Mr Browne** said that he now had very clear evidence that his wife had committed perjury and lied to this court. He had suspected for some time that she was having an affair and he now had evidence of this. Mr Browne had been using the family's computer a few days ago and found a number of emails between Mrs Browne and a man called Andre. These emails had been deleted by Mrs Browne but they were still on the computer.

42. It was clear that she had been having an affair for some months. The emails also showed that Mrs Browne was planning to live with Andre in the future. They intended to pay for their new domestic arrangements with Mr Browne's inheritance seized in the divorce courts. It was not clear what they expected to happen to his children, but the children were obviously a secondary consideration.

43. **Mr Browne** handed copies of the emails to **Judge Upright.**

HUSBAND ANSWERS BARRISTER'S QUESTIONS

44. **Mr Craven** said that it was a pity that Mrs Browne had not brought witnesses with her who could say how unhappy she was with her marriage and, perhaps, confirm some of the statements in her Petition. Would Mr Browne say what had led him on one occasion to bang his hand violently against a wall?

45. **Mr Browne** said that he did not recall any incident like that. He suspected that his wife was exaggerating some minor occurrence to pretend she had a reason to complain.

46. **Mr Craven** asked whether Mr Browne seriously expected the court to believe that Mrs Browne had put the coloured condoms in his jacket pocket?

47. **Mr Browne** replied that he had already said that he had never bought the things. Someone else had put them in his jacket and the only person with a motive to do that was his wife.

48. **Mr Craven** asked whether Mr Browne accepted that he had been unreasonable in making Mrs Browne pay for household expenses when her income was so much smaller than his? This did seem to be evidence that their marriage had broken down irretrievably.

49. **Mr Browne** said that this was not true. He had always given his wife as much as he could afford, but his own income was not large. It was only recently that he had inherited money from his mother and he had been able to be more generous. He had increased

expenditure on most things. However, he had hoped that the family would use his inheritance to move to a larger house, rather than spend the money from day to day.

WIFE'S BARRISTER CONCLUDES

50. **Judge Upright** asked Mr Craven to make a final statement.

51. **Mr Craven** said that Mrs Browne's case was simply that the marriage had broken down irretrievably and that there was ample evidence of that. She did find Mr Browne's behaviour sometimes very difficult and remained convinced that he had a mistress.

52. Mrs Browne herself might never have sought comfort outside her marriage, or made her divorce Petition, if Mr Browne had not given her more help with the children. If he had given her more money over the years, that would also have reduced the pressure on Mrs Browne. She had decided that "the relationship was over" and wanted her fair share of her husband's assets.

HUSBAND CONCLUDES

53. **Mr Browne** said that he had demonstrated that, despite the difficulties, family life continued. There was no convincing evidence of any of the unpleasant allegations that his wife had made in her Petition. She had lied to try to get what she wanted. She should certainly not benefit financially, in any way, by committing perjury.

54. Without the financial incentive to divorce him, he had no doubt that his wife would loose interest in the alternative lifestyle she had planned. Mrs Browne had married him "for better or worse" and, if she wanted to enjoy his property and other assets, she should honour her marriage vow.

55. It was certainly in the children's best interest that a divorce be refused and their family stay together.

Judge Upwright *then retired briefly to consider what he had heard.*

JUDGE UPRIGHT'S DECISION

56. **Judge Upright** said that he had heard the Petitioner's counsel, Mr Craven, and the Respondent, Mr Browne, who had ably represented himself in person. He had seen the papers submitted by the Petitioner's solicitor, which included documents from the Respondent, and had read them all. He had also seen a number of emails brought to the court by Mr Browne.

57. **Judge Upright** said that he had looked carefully at Mrs Browne's allegations of violence but found them unconvincing and lacking in substance. The incidents of which she complained were relatively minor and there was no evidence to corroborate them. He suspected that any domestic conflict was as much of Mrs Browne's making as her husband's.

58. Mrs Browne's allegation that Mr Browne had a sexual relationship with another woman was not proved. Her objection to this was particularly surprising in view of her own conduct. Her claim, under oath, to abhor adultery was false. This was perjury and inevitably cast doubt on the truth of all her other statements to the court.

59. Mr Browne had demonstrated that he had made the greatest financial contribution to the maintenance of his family. This had been the case for many years. His income had been modest for most of the marriage but he could not be blamed for that.

60. **Judge Upright** found that the grounds for divorce given in the Petition were not proved. A decree nisi was refused. Mrs Browne would pay Mr Browne's costs.

61. **Judge Upright** acknowledged that Common Law rights to the ownership of property and family life were paramount. Statutes, made by Parliament, had to be applied consistently so as to leave absolute Common Law rights intact.

62. The European Convention on Human Rights gave modern support for these rights. Mr Browne had been perfectly entitled to remind the court of his fundamental rights.

Written by Ian Browne   Date: 10 December 2004

Signed: *Ian Browne*

ANNEX 9

AN "OPEN POSITION" LETTER

FINANCIAL HEARINGS

- **If your wife gets her divorce, and you cannot reach agreement with her how much of your assets she should get, there will be one or more financial hearings.**

- The first financial hearing is called the Financial Dispute Resolution (FDR). A judge will try to persuade you and your wife to agree a settlement. No settlement will be imposed on you at this hearing.

- If there is no agreement following an FDR, then (after several months) there will be an "Ancillary Relief" hearing. "Ancillary Relief" means that a court makes an order seizing your assets for your wife. (You have a right of appeal.)

WHAT YOU HAVE OFFERED HER

- **Before any financial hearing, you can produce an "open position" letter. This is a letter (addressed to the court or your wife's solicitor) that states what assets you are prepared to give her as a divorce settlement.**

- Your wife can produce a similar "open position" letter stating her demands. The judge will look at these letters at the FDR.

- If your wife does not accept a reasonable settlement that you have put in your "open position" letter, you can later produce the letter as evidence that she has been unreasonable. This may help in persuading a judge that you should not be forced to pay your wife's costs for a financial hearing. (These can be about £2,000.)

- See the example on the next page.

18 Cranberry Close
Turpentown
Berkshire

The Court Manager
The London Family Court
Calumny House
Lawyers' Retreat
London WC2

5 November 2003

Dear Sir,

My wife and I are to attend a Financial Dispute Resolution hearing on 17 November and I am writing to explain my "open position" on the division of assets.

We have no children and our main property is our home. I have always paid the mortgage premiums and most of the household bills. My wife has made only a modest contribution to the essentials of buying and running our home, despite frequent requests from me for help. It is therefore very unreasonable for her to now demand 60% of the property that I alone have paid for. In view of her mean contribution to the purchase of the home, I think that 40% of the equity would be a generous share for her.

I must emphasize that I have an elderly mother who must come to live with me in the near future and I must have adequate accommodation for her in addition to myself. My wife on the other hand will live alone and her needs are less.

My wife and I both work and each has a separate pension. My wife's pension will be adequate for her to maintain herself when she gets to retirement age and, in the meantime, she has plenty of time to build up savings. There is therefore no justification for the seizure of any part of my pension. As she has an adequate income now and in the future, the divorce should be a "clean break" with neither of us being able to demand support from the other.

My wife and I have almost completed the division of household contents into equal shares. I will make a list showing the division of the main items and send a copy to the court soon. We both have our own cars and no change is needed there.

Yours faithfully,

John Charwell

Copied to wife's solicitor.

205

ANNEX 10

A FINANCIAL STATEMENT

IT IS EASIER TO WRITE IT DOWN

- You may not be asked to write a statement about finances.

- But financial matters can be complicated and it may make everything clearer in your mind if you write a detailed statement. You can use the statement as a note to remind you of what to say at a court hearing.

- You should send a copy to the court manager, your solicitor and your wife's solicitor.

AS SHORT OR AS LONG AS YOU LIKE

- You can make your statement short if you want to. It can just refer to the financial declarations that you and your wife have made and say how you think assets should be divided.

- Or, you can put in as many relevant details as you want to.

  These can include :

  i) The background of the divorce and your financial situation.

  ii) Details of your children. (If your wife takes your children, she will demand much more of your assets and future income to provide for them.)

  iii) Your needs for the future and your wife's.

  iv) How you think assets should be divided.

  v) Your comments on your wife's demands.

- See the example of a detailed statement on the next page.

IN THE LONDON FAMILY COURT   No LFC1815/04

Between	CHRISTINE TYLER	Petitioner
And	IAN TYLER	Respondent

RESPONDENT'S FINANCIAL PROPOSALS

BACKGROUND

1. This divorce is the result of my wife's desire to desert me and find a new life for herself. I have been glad to see Christine recover from her anxiety disorder over recent months. Her energy and vigour have returned and she is no longer receiving treatment. However, something decent inside her has died and she no longer cares for her family as she once did. Christine's divorce petition was based on false accusations and she is now presenting an untrue picture of her future accommodation needs and ability to maintain herself. Her primary motive for this deception is material gain, both at my expense and, indirectly, at the expense of our children.

2. Our 4 children are : Edward (18), Suzy (17), James (15) and Larry (12). Edward will leave home in October to go to Pontypridd University - but Suzy and the younger boys will continue at their school in Hammersmith. It is important for the wellbeing of Suzy, James and Larry that they remain with me in the family home after my wife has left. The children were all born into this comfortable home and have lived there all their lives. (James was actually born in the main bedroom.) It would cause them great distress to leave their home at this stage in their development.

LARRY

3. Larry is a sensitive boy and is the youngest and most vulnerable of the children. He is recovering from the recent death of his grandfather, who he was very fond of. With the pressures from the break-up of his family, he has been diagnosed as suffering from depression. He has said consistently for more nearly a year that he will live with his father after the divorce. The residence hearing 3 months ago at the London Family Courts was resolved so that he can do so.

JAMES

4. James has a non-specific food allergy that causes irritating rashes and concentration lapses. He will be taking his GCSEs this year and, if his grades are adequate, will make a brave attempt at A levels. James has had great difficulty in coming to terms with his mother's intention to break-up his family and in deciding which parent he will live with. Christine has said "James is floundering between us." It is selfish and cruel of his mother to encourage him to say that he welcomes leaving his home now.

5. James's current proposal is that he will find accommodation of his own and live with 16 and17 year old friends. As his father and the only psychologically stable adult in his life, I think that this would be disastrous for him and his future would be bleak. Commune life would put an end to his education and lead him into all sorts of other dangers. What he

needs for the next 3 or 4 years is the safety net of a stable and disciplined home where he can recover from the turbulence that he has lived with in the recent past. If Suzy, Larry and I stay in our home, then I have no doubt that James will be glad to remain with us until his education is complete.

SUZY

6. Suzy is mature for her age and takes an adult interest in the welfare of her younger brothers. She agrees with me that it is best for them that they stay in the home where they feel secure. Suzy intends to study Product Design at a London college when she leaves school and so our present home will be an ideal base for her. She hopes that her mother will not be far away so that all the children can see her regularly.

THE FUTURE

7. My ability to sustain our home for the children depends on my wife's financial demands not being excessive. I therefore propose that I obtain a bank loan for several years, of £90,000, to be paid to my wife so that she can buy another property to live in by herself. (I have made enquiries with lenders and this is viable.) My wife has not made any contribution to the purchase of our present home over 19 years, despite often having the means to do so and sometimes seeing me in financial difficulties. I think that this settlement is fair.

8. Christine is now free to work full-time and can do so without difficulty. She has demonstrated this by taking a part-time job while looking after her family and helping a local charity. When her domestic responsibilities are less, she will have the time and energy to increase her earnings. She is, however, holding back at present to give a false impression of future hardship.

9. I think that Christine will find herself living alone after the divorce. Edward will be away studying engineering, which will permit only short, infrequent visits home. Suzy, even if she were persuaded to join her mother initially, would soon return to her brothers. Larry has always been adamant that he will live with his father and James will follow suit.

10. Christine has for most of the past 12 months said that she will go to live in Northampton. She has said that she hates Hammersmith and has not been able to find the kind of property that she likes there. I suspect that she will indeed go to Northampton after the divorce. None of the children want to go with her despite what the "Welfare Officer" said in her report.

11. I have kept my family and our home together for many years under difficult conditions. The children and I stood by Christine when she was ill and we do not deserve what she is doing to us now. My wife's present financial demands are greatly in excess of what she needs or what I can accept. I have said to Christine that I will appeal against any decision which does not allow me to sustain the family home - even though this might take us to the European Court. This does not appear to concern her.

12. It is important that the continuing damage to my children by my wife's divorce is stopped as soon as possible. The special circumstances of my family deserve special consideration. I trust that it will be possible to resolve this unhappy affair satisfactorily for us all at the hearing on 18 April.

RESPONDENT'S PROPOSALS

My proposals for the financial settlement are :

Property

13. My property is the family home which is in my name. My wife and I have both made an equal contribution in money's worth to the home but I alone have paid for it over 19 years. During the whole of this time, my wife has persistently refused to make any contribution to the monthly mortgage premiums or the household bills, despite having the means to help.

14. The home has been recently valued by an independent valuer at £300,000.

The home has also been valued by various local estate agents at between £250,000 and £350,000 (giving an average of £300,000).

There is a mortgage on the property of £70,000.

Proposal

15. I propose that the home should remain my property, together with fixtures, fittings, carpets and curtains.

I will obtain a loan of £90,000 to give to my wife as the basis for a clean break. She has 25 years of full time employment in front of her and will be able to finance a mortgage of £80,000. This will allow her to buy another property for herself where the children can visit her. It is a misleading falsehood for her to claim that she is now not able to work full time.

Furniture and Household Items

Proposal

16. I think that it is fair that all furniture and household items be divided equally between my wife and me. We may need a valuation of the main items before we do this. I do not foresee any difficulty but we more time for discussion and this cannot be resolved in Court on 18 April. We will send a list, signed by both of us, to the Court soon.

Pension

17. I have an occupational pension from Composite Chemicals PLC and my wife has one from the Acumen Entertainment Ltd.

Proposal

Although the current valuation of my pension is larger than hers, she is younger than I am and has many years in which to build hers up. Therefore, none of my pension should be taken for her.

Motor Cars

18. My wife has her car and I have mine.

Proposal

No change is needed.

Maintenance

19. My wife is barely halfway through her working life and has a greater future earning capacity than I have :

She will earn a gross income of £30,000 pa for the next 25 years - giving a total earning capacity of £750,000.

I have a gross income of £35,000 pa until I retire in 11 years time - giving a total earning capacity of £385,000. (This may be substantially reduced by health concerns.)

My wife's assertion that she cannot earn more than £15,000 pa is simply untrue. She now has the energy and time to pursue her career in the entertainment industry and I attach a copy of current pay scales. Christine also has experience of managing a personnel agency. Therefore, she may well have the opportunity to earn substantially more than £30,000 pa in the future.

Proposal

20. I do not seek any maintenance for myself from my wife and she does not need any from me. She is a woman with a lot of experience in different occupations and is now well able to work full time to maintain herself. All my resources will be deployed to maintain the home and family that my wife is deserting. I have, over the years, earned some respite from this lady's demands.

Any child support issues may best be left to the Child Support Agency.

Savings and Investments

21. I have none, except £30 in the Post Office and £110 in the Solid Rock Building Society.

COMMENTS ON WIFE'S FINANCIAL PROPOSALS

22. My wife's divorce petition was founded on false claims and her present financial demands are also dishonest. She is now understating her future earning capacity, denying her future opportunities for increasing her pension and greatly exaggerating her future accommodation needs.

My comments on my wife's financial demands (received in a letter) are :

Property

23. My property is the family home which is in my name and which I alone have paid for over 20 years. My wife has always refused any contribution to the cost of either buying the home or the monthly household bills despite often having the income to do so.

My wife's claim that the property is worth £360,000 is greatly exaggerated :

The independent expert valuer said that it was worth £300,000.

Various local estate agents have valued it at between £250,000 and £350,000 - also giving an average of £300,000.

I suspect that the true value is a little less.

My wife's claim that she needs a 4 bedroom property to accommodate her and 3 children is not true. Christine will almost certainly be living by herself for most of the time. Edward will be studying engineering in Pontypridd and making short infrequent visits. Suzy, if she attempts to live with her mother, will not do so for long. Larry has been adamant from the beginning that he will live with his father - and so will James.

I have offered to obtain a loan of £90,000 to give to my wife. She is able to work full time and, with an income of £30,000 pa, will have no difficulty in obtaining a mortgage of £80,000 to buy a comfortable home.

Small Legacy

24. My wife has complained that I have spent all the small legacy of £16,000 that I received just over a year ago. I have given a detailed schedule of the expenditure of this money in a letter to my wife's solicitor. This demonstrated responsible use of the money, for the benefit of my family: holidays, clothes, a computer, treats for the children and extra household expenditure.

In the difficult circumstances into which my wife has forced us, the money could not have been spent better. It is absurd for my wife to demand that the money should be deemed to still be mine.

Pension

25. My wife has had constant encouragement to build a bigger pension - but despite a generous income for many years has fecklessly preferred to spend money. This means that she has lost a large amount in employers' contributions. There is no reason why her extravagance should be rewarded by giving her some of my pension as she demands.

Income

26. My wife has recovered from her recent illness. She has regained her capacity to work full time and, as a member of an established profession, is able to earn at least £30,000 pa. She is at present holding back on work to give the Court a false impression of her earning potential. This is not honest.

Savings

27. The only savings that I have now are £30 in the Post Office and £110 in the Solid Rock Building Society.

Demands for Money

28. The demand for 60% of my property is grossly unreasonable. I am over 54 years old, with at most 11 years left to work. My wife has 25 years before she is required to retire and has a substantially greater future earning capacity than I have. (Hers is £750,000 gross and mine is at most £385,000.) I have told my wife that such demands could take us to the European Court, with all that entails, but she does not seem concerned.

It is also absurd to expect me to take on a mortgage of £90,000 at the age of 54.

Maintenance

29. In view of my wife having a much greater future earning capacity than I, it is not appropriate that I should be required to pay her maintenance in the future. I will have children and their home to support - her monthly expenditure will be much less and her own income ample for her needs.

There is therefore no case for giving her a nominal maintenance order so that she can demand money from me in the future. Such a measure would remove any incentive that she has to provide herself with a pension and act with financial responsibility. She is fully able to provide for herself in the future and I have earned the right to be free of such a burden.

Children

30. I have explained above that it is probable that my wife will live alone in future.

Edward (18) will be in Pontypridd and is an adult. Any support for him is a private matter for discussion between him and his parents. Suzy, James and Larry will live with their father.

Ian Tyler   11 October 2003

Copied to wife's solicitor.

ANNEX 11

A FINANCIAL HEARING RECORD

WRITE DOWN WHAT HAS BEEN DONE TO YOU

- The purpose of financial court hearings is to seize your assets, or income, for your wife. (This is called "Ancillary Relief".) The court will later send you a court order which states very briefly what has been seized from you.

- **The judge gives his decision on what assets are to be seized from you, at the end of a hearing. It is important that you make your own detailed notes of what he says. (Take plenty of notepaper with you.)**

YOU NEED A PROPER RECORD

- **After the hearing, you should use your notes to write a statement of what the judge decided. This will be your only detailed written record of what has been done to you.**

- Your wife's solicitor may employ a clerk to make a written record of the judge's decision. You should ask for a copy. Tell her if there are any inaccuracies or omissions. (As an alternative to writing your own statement, you may be able to agree an amended version of the clerk's record.)

- **You will need a detailed written record of the judge's decision on finances if you decide to appeal.**

- See the example on the next page.

IN THE LONDON FAMILY COURT   No LFC1413/2004

Between   **JENNIFER   LOBB**   **Petitioner**

And   **ARTHUR   LOBB**   **Respondent**

FINANCIAL HEARING

JUDGE BLACKHEART'S FINDINGS

CALUMNY HOUSE, LONDON ON 12 OCTOBER 2003

1. District Judge Blackheart said that he had heard oral evidence from the wife's barrister and the husband in person.

1.1 The Judge said that he had read :   the trial bundle, the husband's Answer to the Petition, child residence documents, a statement by the husband and further documents given at Court. He had heard the oral evidence of 2 property valuers.

1.2 A decree nisi had been issued in June 2003 after a long marriage. The children were Simon 15 and Andrew nearly 13. The husband, wife and children all lived in the matrimonial home which was in the husband's name.

1.3 There had been contested child residence proceedings at the London Family Court on 17 May 2003, conceded by the wife, and much discussion about where the 2 children will live. It was agreed that Andrew would live with his father but Simon's future was less certain.

2. CHILD RESIDENCE

2.1 Judge Blackheart's findings were that :

2.2 Simon has just taken his GCSEs and might then go on to take A levels. He was not academically gifted but would probably be in full time education for the foreseeable future. He wanted to stay at Hornblowers School. The Judge accepted the wife's claim that she had given up her ambition to live in Newcastle which would have been an unsuitable move for Simon.

2.3 Simon had told a Welfare Officer that he would probably live with his mother and a letter, written by the wife and signed by Simon, indicated the same. There had been several recent aggressive arguments between the wife and Simon but the Judge accepted the wife's evidence that he would live with her.

2.4 As agreed in the High Court in May, Andrew would have his main home with his father and probably stay with the wife from time to time. The Welfare Officer said that he might share his time between the two, although the husband disputed the WO's report.

3. HOUSING NEEDS

3.1 The Judge said that both parents would have the same housing needs to look after children.

3.2 The wife needed 3 bedrooms so that Andrew would have a room whenever he visited his mother.

3.3 The husband also needed 3 bedrooms so that Simon could visit and stay with him. The Welfare Officer stressed that the children should spend time in each other's company. Andrew was depressed, unhappy at school and had been injured playing rugby last month. Simon was important to him.

3.4 The wife had said that the husband's housing needs were less than hers but this was not the case.

4. MAINTENANCE

4.1 Simon and Andrew could not be provided with maintenance except by consent. There was no jurisdiction to provide for maintenance except by a global order (Dawney Kingdom).

4.2 The wife had not asked for maintenance at present but demanded a nominal order as a means of getting it in the future.

5. HUSBAND'S FINANCIAL POSITION

5.1 The husband was a Business Manager in British Petroleum.

5.2 His P60 to April 2003 showed an income of £49,500.22 and the Judge accepted that his income for the next year would be a little over £50,000 gross and £32,930 net (less superannuation).

5.3 The husband's car had been stolen recently and he had £12,500 insurance money from this.

5.4 He had £80 in saving certificates and his British Petroleum pension was given a paper value of £145,000 in January 2003.

5.5 He owed £1,500 in solicitor's charges.

6. WIFE'S FINANCIAL POSITION

6.1 The Judge found that the wife's earnings in the past year had been reduced by illness and did not reflect what she could earn in the forthcoming year.

6.2 The wife could earn £15,560 gross and £12,467 net in the forthcoming year.

6.3 She had little capital but a car which she said was worth £4,000 and jewellery worth £3,000

6.4 She owed a modest amount on several credit cards.

6.5 She had spent £18,850 in legal aid.

7. VALUATION OF THE FAMILY HOME

7.1 The Judge had heard the oral reports of two valuers (one for each party) but found it impossible to say which of them was right.

7.2 Mr Spears had said in writing that the home was worth £500,000 (but might now be worth £525,000). He had 35 years experience in Kennington.

7.3 Mr Hayek valued the property at £450,000. He had 2 years experience in Kennington and before had covered the whole of the South of England. He had conducted comprehensive research but this was not to say that Mr Spears had not.

7.4 There was no meeting of minds and there was some criticism of Mr Spears for not agreeing to a meeting to compromise. There must have been a misunderstanding between the two men. Both had seen each other's comparables and each could be right or wrong. The true value may be in the middle of the valuers' figures and was not less than £450,000.

7.5 The husband had also obtained estate agents valuations and the lowest was £375,000. It appeared to be a difficult property to value and the market was still rising.

8. WIFE'S EARNING CAPACITY

8.1 The Judge referred to the wife's career history and temporary work that she had taken while bringing up a family.   It was 5 years ago that she had become an aroma therapist. In April 2001, she had become ill and had to take time off.

8.2 The wife had returned to work in September 2001 and had since been building up her income to £15,500 pa. The Judge accepted all her evidence about this. The wife's maximum earning capacity was deemed to be £25,000 pa but it was not possible to say when she would achieve that but perhaps soon after these proceedings. The maximum of that an aroma therapist could expect to earn was £30,000 pa but the wife cannot earn at that rate.

9. WIFE'S ILLNESS

9.1 The Judge had read a report by a psychiatrist from Funnifarms Sanatorium which said that the wife had suffered a significant depressive episode and this was not challenged by the husband. He went further saying that the wife had a history of schizophrenia and she had recovered from very severe mental illness.

9.2 The Judge thought that the wife could not work more than she was now and would work a maximum of 30 hours a week in the future given her vulnerability to illness. There should therefore not be a clean break order now and there would be a nominal periodic payments order for an indefinite period. It was possible that this could be changed to a clean break in the future.

10. MONEY FROM UNIT TRUSTS

10.1 In February 2002, the husband received £32,654 from his unit trusts and he alone decided how to spend it. Unlike previous savings, this money was not spent on reducing the mortgage on the home. The husband chose to spend the money on a car, repaying loans, redecorating the home, family holidays, a computer, a music centre, solicitor's fees, medical fees, children's entertainment and £8,931 on household expenses.

10.2 It had not been unreasonable to buy a car but the husband should have used about £12,000 from the savings to reduce the mortgage.

10.3 Previously in 2001, the husband had taken out a loan of £16,000 to set up a small trading company which failed. The loss of £7,143 was paid out of the unit trust proceeds. Judge Blackheart did not criticize him for a failed business.

11. THE OBJECT OF THE PROCEEDINGS

11.1 The Judge said the object of the proceedings was to achieve a fair outcome, taking into consideration the interests of two minor children and the provisions of the Matrimonial Causes Act. He had checked the "yardstick of equality", so that there was no discrimination against the home-maker (taking into consideration White and White and also Cowan and Cowan).

11.2 There was no evidence that either party would have other resources in the future and it was clear that the husband had already reached his maximum earning capacity.

12. HOUSING

12.1 Husband and wife had like needs in the future. The Judge had looked at estate agents' material for properties in the range £160-220,000 and these could meet the basic needs of both parties. Neither party had asked for more capital than was required for their housing needs.

12.2 The husband was able to fully maintain himself and the wife was able to fully maintain herself.

12.3 Their standard of living while married had often been modest, with the husband earning £30-50,000 and the wife earning £10-15,000. Nevertheless, the family home was delightful and to the credit of both. They had both worked hard to achieve this. The Judge had taken into account the ages of the parties. The husband had no health problems and the wife was physically fit but had a history of emotional problems and there would therefore be no clean break.

12.4 The Judge found that both parties had made their maximum contribution to the marriage. The husband had worked full time and often cared for the two children when his wife was not available. The wife had worked part time, done gardening and kept the home. The husband had understated the wife's contribution and it had to be accepted that her income had been for the benefit of the family.

12.5 Both parties will contribute to the care of the children in the next few years. The husband will look after Andrew and the wife will keep Simon. Both husband and wife will work. Although the wife was at present still vulnerable due to her emotional problems.

13. GENERAL CONDUCT

13.1 Allegations had been made by the husband about violent conduct by the wife, "both obvious and gross", but these had not been tested as the divorce suit had eventually gone forward undefended. The Judge therefore decided that no conduct by either party was relevant to ancillary relief.

14. PENSIONS

14.1 The husband had a pension. The wife had no pension despite persistent encouragement from her husband and others. She could not be criticized for that because she had always had many things to spend her income on.

14.2 50% of the husband's pension would therefore be seized for his wife. The cost of the transfer would be divided equally.

15. EQUITY IN THE FAMILY HOME

15.1 It had to be decided whether the family home should be sold or the husband granted his wish to retain his property for the children and borrow money to pay off his wife. The evidence from the valuers indicated that the home was worth between £450,000 and £525,000.

15.2 The husband had described the home as having 4 bedrooms, 2 bathrooms and 3 reception rooms. His open position was an offer of a payment of £130,000 to his wife but he had indicated several times to his wife's solicitors that this figure was negotiable. He had submitted evidence that he could borrow £140,000 for this purpose. He had therefore provided evidence that he could pay what he had offered but no evidence that he could pay more.

15.3 It was his proposal that he would obtain a loan large enough to cover interest payments and repay the total debt when he sold the property after the boys' had completed their education in several years' time. This was a high-risk strategy, which made him vulnerable if house prices fell but it was a risk that he was prepared to take.

15.4 The Judge decided that £130,000 was not sufficient to provide the wife with a home as her mortgage capacity was limited (and not £90,000 as the husband suggested). When the wife reached her maximum gross earning capacity of £25,000 pa she would still struggle to meet mortgage payments. The husband does not need such a substantial home in the future.

15.5 The Judge decided that the family home should be sold. If the property realized £500,000, then the equity would be £390,500 after costs. If Mr Spears's higher valuation were correct, then the equity would be £415,500. The Judge decided that 55% of the equity should be paid to the wife and 45% to the husband. The wife's open proposal that she should get 75% would not be fair as there was not to be a clean break at present.

15.6 The Judge thought that the husband could afford a mortgage of £100,000 in the future, even though he had expected to retire in a few years. Assuming that his home sold for £500,000, he would receive £175,725 (45%) of the equity, which would allow him to buy a new property similar to the one that his wife could buy with a modest mortgage. £100,000 was less than the short-term loan that he was prepared to borrow to keep his present home for the children.

15.7 The Judge said that it would not be equitable for the husband to keep 50% of his property. The wife had a need to buy a new home with only a modest mortgage, while the husband's future income allowed him to take on further debt. The wife was vulnerable because of her emotional difficulties and lower income.

15.8 Leaving aside cars and small capital, the equity in the home and husband's pension fund totalled £535,500. An award to the wife of 55% of the equity in the home gave her £214,775 and, including 50% her husband's pension, 53.6% of the global figure. If the higher valuation of the property were realized, 55% of the husband's property for the wife would give her £228,525 and with a similar percentage of the global figure. Both figures were fair.

15.9 The conduct of the sale of the husband's property was to be given to the wife. An order for sale would be a disappointment for the husband but he had contemplated its sale when he spoke to the Welfare Officer. He must accept the realities of divorce in this country. There was to be a clean break as far as maintenance for the husband was concerned. He would never be able to claim maintenance from the wife.

16. HOUSE CONTENTS

16.1 The parties would agree a division of contents between them and the matter would be referred back to the Court after agreement.

17. DISPOSAL OF FAMILY HOME

17.1 The Judge decided that the husband would pay a lump sum to the wife.

This to be raised as follows:

17.2 The family home 11 Gracefield Street, Kennington, at present the property of the husband, would be seized and sold on the open market forthwith.

17.3 The property would be sold at an initial asking price of £525,000.

17.4 The wife would conduct the sale and her solicitor would do the conveyancing.

17.5 The property would be sold through ABC estate agents.

17.6 The proceeds of the sale would be used to :

    a)   Discharge the current mortgage to the Abbey National plc

    b)   Pay the wife's solicitors' conveyancing fees

    c)   Pay estate agents fees

d) Pay 55% to the wife with the balance to the husband.

18. NOMINAL MAINTENANCE

18.1 From the date of this hearing the husband would pay the wife £1 pa as maintenance. This would allow her to return to court at any time in the future to demand real maintenance. The husband would never be able to claim maintenance from the wife.

18.2 Current claims for further maintenance were dismissed.

18.3 The husband shall not be entitled to apply for an order under Section 2.

19. COSTS

19.1 The husband had only offered the wife a payment of £130,000. However, he did tell her solicitors twice at the Financial Dispute Resolution hearing that this figure was negotiable. It was a pity that the wife's solicitors did not take up this offer to negotiate, which might have resulted in an equitable settlement, but this was only a slight criticism of them.

19.2 The husband was therefore ordered to pay 75% of the wife's costs for this "Ancillary Relief" hearing.

19.3 The Judge thought that it was relevant that when the husband made his financial declaration, on Form E, he did not give details of a failed investment through NatWest Bank which resulted in a loss of £6,478 between March 2000 and June 2001.

19.4 The wife's legal team would prepare a schedule of their costs for the husband's perusal and detailed assessment. There may be a separate Court hearing to decide what the husband should be compelled to pay the wife's lawyers.

19.5 The husband said that he would appeal against such an unjust settlement based on a divorce Petition that contained perjury. He said that his wife was motivated to seek a divorce partly by her emotional problems and by the prospect of seizing large assets paid for entirely by her husband. He said that he strongly objected to the conduct of this court in secret without the scrutiny of the press. Secret courts always produced secret injustice.

Arthur Lobb

ANNEX 12

A NOTICE OF APPEAL

TO APPEAL OR NOT APPEAL ?

- **You can appeal against any court order that you think is unjust.**

- **You can base your appeal on information that the first judge knew about, or you can ask if you can produce new evidence (or both).**

- Ask your solicitor which court you should appeal to and your chance of success. Ask him which laws are relevant to your appeal. These may include the Matrimonial Causes Act 1973 and the Human Rights Act 1998. You may want to get copies from The Stationery Office (OPSI) (tel: 0870 600 5522).

- Remember that if you loose an appeal, your wife will demand that you pay her lawyers' bill for that hearing. She may take the opportunity, at your appeal, to change her own demands.

HOW TO APPEAL

- **Obtain the right appeal form.** Your solicitor may have one or you can telephone the court office of the court to which you are appealing. (Ask what fee must be sent with the appeal.)

- Fill in the form with all the information asked for, including : the order you are appealing against, what you want to happen instead and your grounds for appealing.

- **Your appeal (and the fee) must reach the court before a deadline (often 7 or 14 days after the date on the order). Do not miss the deadline.**

- See the example of an appeal form on the next page.

G3(b) District judge to judge (final order) (county court)

Notice of appeal from final order or order treated as final by virtue of FPR 1991, r 8.1(2) (which includes appeals against ancillary relief orders) or from an interlocutory or final order under the Children Act 1989.

G3-031

In the _____ County Court

No. of Matter _____

Between _____   Applicant

and

_____   Respondent

TAKE NOTICE THAT the _____ intends to apply to the Judge of this Court at

_____ on _____ day the _____ day of _____ 20_____ at _____ o'clock for an order that the order made on _____ 20_____ by District Judge _____ whereby it was ordered that

[state the order appealed against]

be set aside and that

[state order sought].

AND TAKE NOTICE that the grounds of this application are:

[state grounds]

DATED this _____ day of _____ 20_____ .

_____

Solicitors for the

_____

To the Chief Clerk of the _____ County Court
and to the _____ and to [his/her] solicitors   *[G3-041 follows]*

222

ANNEX 13

A LETTER TO YOUR MP (and MEP)

THE NEED FOR CHANGE

- **The long term solution to the injustice that the Divorce Courts inflict on men and their children is new legislation.**

- The present system must be pulled down and replaced with laws and courts that respect the rights of men and children.

TWO LETTERS

- **If you want change, write to your Member of Parliament (and also your Member of the European Parliament). You can include a copy of "The 9 Principles for Reform" if you want to.**

- Explain that the present abuse of human rights, in corrupt courts, is not acceptable and that you want your Member to take the lead in making new laws.

- Your MP's address is :

  The House of Commons
  London SW1A 0AA.

- Your MEP's address is :

  The European Parliament
  47-53 Rue Wiertz
  B-1047 Brussels
  Belgium.

- See the example of a letter on the next page.

Shangri-La
Assam Drive
Bognor Regis

Mr B Terne MP
House of Commons
Westminster
London SW1A 0AA

25 October 2003

Dear Mr Terne

I would be grateful for your urgent action on the most important human rights issue in this country today.

For a generation, Divorce Courts have abused the most fundamental rights of men and children. Now, 70% of divorces are obtained by wives deserting their husbands. The main reason for this imbalance is the large and unjustified financial incentives which are offered to women to break up their families. There is also the presumption that a divorcing wife will take a man's children from him.

As a result of the State's promotion of divorce by women, the United Kingdom has the highest divorce rate of any West European country. Our divorce rate is 50% higher than the average for the EU. This causes terrible damage to 150,000 British children every year and the ruin of a very large number of honest men. There is no precedent in recent history for the seizure of assets and the separation of children from their parent on this scale.

I would like you to take the lead in Parliament to start urgent reform of the unjust and destructive Divorce Courts. I would be grateful if you would begin by writing to all relevant government departments, and other bodies, urging an immediate review of the whole of the divorce system.

Please will you pursue these arguments :

1. An unlawful system of divorce on demand exists. It is used to abuse men's basic rights to property and parenthood under the European Convention on Human Rights, the Human Rights Act 1998 and the Common Law of England.

2. Perjury by women demanding divorce is accepted by English judges every day. False judgements are common. This is the courts' normal basis for business. These courts are corrupt.

3. Theft by divorce of the property of honest men is the incentive for women to destroy their families. This is why 70% of divorces are now obtained by women.

4. Children are seized from their fathers. To deny men the right to bring up their children is a gross abuse of men's rights.

5. Children are denied the right to a stable and secure home with their father. This is a gross abuse of children's rights. 150,000 children are damaged, for the rest of their lives by the Divorce Courts, every year.

6. Secret courts are always unjust. The press and public are not allowed into most Divorce Courts. Without scrutiny there is always injustice. All courts should be open to all whether those involved ask for it or not. Injustice must be seen <u>not</u> to be done.

7. The Legal Aid system discriminates against men in divorce cases. Men in work are usually refused Legal Aid and cannot claim costs from a wife who has it. A wife has a bottomless purse to pay lawyers, while her husband is impoverished.

8. Inflated legal costs are forced onto men to deter them from appealing against injustice. A wife's lawyers are allowed to more than double their bill whenever the husband is made to pay her costs. This old Spanish practice must cease.

I would like to tell you briefly my own experience of this wicked system:…………………………..

As one of your constituents, I hope that you will agree that this is the most important social reform that Parliament must now address. It must be given the highest priority.

I would like you to use all your determination and influence to bring about the urgent and long overdue reform of the unjust and corrupt divorce system. New laws are needed without delay.

I look forward to hearing from you soon that you have started to take action. Please send me regular reports on progress.

Yours sincerely,

Jack Clarke

ANNEX 14

A MESSAGE TO THE DIVORCE INDUSTRY

THE CURSE OF THE INFIGHTER

- The occult is an underused resource in our society.

  It is interesting how the invocation of the supernatural catches the imagination.

  A curse is often remembered long after rational ideas are forgotten.

- If you want to smite your enemies, consider a well crafted curse.

  Those who beset you in the divorce industry may be unnerved by it.

  And, if they find themselves suffering from incontinence, barrenness and a dose of the pox, it is probably no more than they deserve.

- **A curse can be delivered in person or in writing.**

  A simple example is :

  "I curse you for the evil that you have done to me and to my children.

  May fate have something very unpleasant waiting for you.

  I curse you."

- You may want to be more creative.

  Voodoo is a rich vein of the black arts.

…ooo ☺ ooo…

INDEX / GLOSSARY

divorce. 220

Ancillary Relief Order 222
The final court order on finance providing ancillary relief.

Annulment (or Nullity) 159-165
A court decision that a marriage is not, or never was, a proper or valid marriage.

Answer 13, 16, **17**, 24, 2
The written reply, to a court, that a Respondent makes in answer to a divorce 26, 28, 29, 34, 3
Petition. 39, 43, 65, 80, 8
An "Answer" must arrive at the court within a time limit (usually 28 days). 82, 93, 97, 170,
175, **177**, 196

Anti-stalking Order
A court order preventing one person from harassing, intimidating or threatening
another.

Appeal 28, **37**, 70, **72**, 8
A request to a higher court to cancel, or change, an order made by a lower court. 3, 91-4, 97-9, 1(
196, 204, 213, **2**

Appeal Court 37, 52, 72-5, 91
An appeal against an order by a District judge is heard by a Circuit judge. The
Court of Appeal hears appeals against decisions by a Circuit judge. Appeals against
decisions of the Court of Appeal go to the House of Lords. Permission to appeal
is sometimes needed.

Application 83, **97**, 115-6, 1
A written request to a court to make an order. The court office has a form for this, 131,162, 222
and there is a fee.

Arrears
The total value of forced payments, ordered by a court in the past, that have not
been paid.

Asset 21, 25, 27, 33, 3
Anything that has value, such as: a house, pension, cash, car, jewellery, furniture or **36-42**, 45, 47, 5(
shares. **65-9**, 133, 143-(
147, 184, 204, 2(
213

Attachment of Earnings Order
A court order forcing an employer to send a part of someone's earnings to
someone else (usually to his former wife).

Barrister (or Counsel) 44, 70, 73, 80,
102, 166, 197
An expensive lawyer whom solicitors sometimes get to represent a client in court

Blackstone 8, 167, 230
Sir William Blackstone, the 18th century English judge whose "Commentaries on
the Laws of England" is the most important statement of the rights and freedoms
of the English people, and their Constitution.

Brief
A document giving all the information on a case.

CAFCASS Officer
See "Welfare Officer".

Calderbank Letter
A letter making a financial offer to settle a divorce. (Only to be shown to the judge after he has decided what the settlement should be.) The purpose of the letter is to show that the other person has been unreasonable, in not accepting the offer, and should pay costs.

Capital Gains Tax
A tax that is sometimes paid on the profit made when a substantial asset is sold or transferred to someone else.

Care and Attention
An item in a solicitor's bill for work done, and time spent, on a case.

Care Order
A court order giving a local authority responsibility for a child, and sometimes power to take the child from his family.

Cash Equivalent Transfer Value (CETV)
The total cash value of all the contributions that have been paid into someone's pension fund, over the years.

Chambers
"In Chambers" is a secret court. The Public and Press are kept out to conceal what the court is doing. You should always ask for them to be admitted.

Charge on Property
The right to get some of the money when property is sold.

Charging Order
A court order forcing the payment of a debt against property. For example, a house might have to be sold to pay off the mortgage.

Chattels
House contents and personal effects (furniture, curtains, jewellery, clothes etc).

Child Assessment Order
A court order for the medical assessment of a child.

Child Benefit
A State benefit paid to a person who cares for a child, until the child is 16 (or 19 if in full-time education).

Child Residence
Arrangements for a child to live with a particular person after a divorce or separation.
Also called "Custody".

Child Support (or Child Maintenance)
Regular forced payments by one parent to the other for the needs of a child. This usually continues until the child finishes secondary education, but can be extended to cover further education.

Child Support Act 1991 (as amended)
The Act that transferred responsibility for deciding financial support for children from the courts to the Child Support Agency.

Child Support Agency
This government body calculates and collects forced payments from men not living with their children. It issues leaflets explaining what it does and is universally despised.

Children's Guardian
A CAFCASS Officer, or "Welfare Officer", appointed by a court to represent a child, usually against a parent's wishes.

Chronology
A list, in date order, of the main events in a marriage, leading to a divorce Petition, prepared for a court.

Class F
A procedure for forcing a wife's demand to live in her husband's property, if it is not registered at the Land Registry.

Clean Break
A divorce where neither the man, nor the woman, will ever have to pay maintenance for the other. This should remove any future threat to income, capital, property, pension and inheritance.

Closed Position
A "closed position" is any proposals you have about a financial settlement for divorce, that you have not yet told your wife. An "open position" is an offer of a financial settlement put in a letter to your wife, before a court hearing.

Commentaries
Sir William Blackstone, the 18th century English judge, wrote the "Commentaries on the Laws of England" which is the finest statement of the rights and freedoms of the English people; and their Constitution.

Common Law
The rights, freedoms, customs and principles of justice of the English people, developed as rules of social conduct for more than a millennium, establishing open courts using trial by jury.

Common Law Marriage
A popular term for a couple living together but not married. It has no legal force in England.

Community Legal Service   77
A scheme provided by the Legal Services Commission to provide advice and legal aid to some people for court cases, such as divorce.

Conciliation   29, 43
Agreement on finance, children or anything else.
(Reconciliation is deciding not to divorce, and continue with the marriage.)

Contempt of Court   91, 105
The deliberate refusal to observe a court decision, or expressing scorn for a judge. They can penalize you for this.

Consent Order
A court order made with the agreement of both parties.

Contested Divorce   12, 13, **14**, 24, 29
A divorce where the Respondent, who has received a divorce Petition, has put in an   31, 38, 41, **44**, 52
"Answer" saying that the grounds for divorce are false and he contests the divorce.   65, 80, 82, **175**,
                                                                           177, **196**

Contact   57, 64, 146
Contact (or access) is the right to visit a child who lives with someone else, or to take the child out, or on holiday, or to have the child to stay temporarily.

Contact Order
A court order saying what contact a particular person can have with a child.

Co-habitation
An man and woman permanently living together without marrying.

Co-respondent   49, 174
A person with whom a Respondent is said to have committed adultery (had sex).

Costs   15, 18, 21, 39, 41,
Fees charged by solicitors (and barristers). Men are often forced to pay their wife's 53, 67, 69, 70, 77,
costs, even when she has Legal Aid.   79, **80**, **82**, 84, 92,
                                                                           97, 100, 102,
                                                                           104,106,
                                                                           122, 129, 128, 204

Court of Appeal
See Appeal Court

Court Order   27, 37, 56, 62, 83,
A document written by a judge that is legally binding on someone.   86, 97, 149, 213,
                                                                           221

Counsel
A barrister who may represent a client in court, or gives an expert opinion on

231

something.

County Court
A court that deals with most divorce cases.

Cross-examination
The questioning of someone taking part in court proceedings by a lawyer representing someone else. Or questioning of someone by a person who is representing himself.

Cross Petition
A divorce Petition, made by someone who has received a Petition himself, asking for a divorce, but giving different reasons for the breakdown of the marriage.

Custody
The right to care for and keep a child. Also called "Child Residence".

Decree Absolute
A court order saying that a marriage is at an end. Both parties are then free to remarry.

Decree Nisi
A court order saying that a decree absolute may be issued in 6 weeks (or later). Once a decree nisi is issued, assets can be seized and redistributed.

Deed
A legal document that is signed, sealed and delivered by the person who writes it

Deduction from Earnings Order
An order from the Child Support Agency forcing an employer to pay a part of someone's earnings to the CSA.

Default Judgement
An order, or decision, by a court after hearing one party only, because the other party failed to respond, or did not respond within a time limit, or did not come to court.

Defendant (or Respondent)
A person who is being sued in court. Usually called the Respondent in "family" courts.

Department for Constitutional Affairs
This government department : appoints judges, administers the courts and Legal Aid, and proposes changes to the law.

Desertion
The abandoning of one spouse by the other, without the consent of the first. To be grounds for divorce, they must live apart for at least 2 years.

Directions
Instructions given by a judge in a divorce case.

Directions for Trial
Instructions by a judge for information to be given, so that the information (called evidence) can be "tried" at a later hearing.

Disbursements
Payments made by a solicitor on behalf of a client, then claimed back from the client.

Disclosure 85, 113, 187
The demand for information, usually financial, for divorce proceedings.

Discovery
Information and documents (usually about finance) that someone is forced to give to someone else during a divorce.

Dissolution 117, 164
A divorce.

District Judge 28, 44
The most junior kind of judge who deals with divorce cases. Often they are only high street solicitors.

Divorce Petition 3, 13, **14**, **15**, 16,
The first document issued by a court in a divorce case. It is signed by the **17**, 24, **25**, 38, 41,
Petitioner who wants a divorce and sent to the Respondent. 47, 65, 69, 80, 82,
91, 97, 102,
159, **170**, **171**

Divorce Suit Hearing 26, 29, **31**, 38,
The Divorce Suit Hearing is the court hearing, in a contested divorce, at which the **44**, 82, **196**,
Petitioner tries to prove her grounds for a divorce, and the Respondent tries to 197
disprove them. A judge then decides whether there will be a divorce.

Domicile
A permanent home.

Duxbury Calculation
A formula, used by judges, to calculate a lump sum a husband will be forced to pay a wife instead of paying maintenance. It is based on the maintenance she would have got and for how long.

Earmarking
A part of the pension lump sum, that a man will receive on retirement, is seized for his wife.

Equity 77, 86, 185, 205,
The value of a home, if it were sold, after deducting the mortgage, solicitor's fees, 217
estate agent's fees and other costs.

First Directions Appointment (FDA)
A first hearing about financial matters, so that the judge can decide what information will be demanded about assets and anything else.

Form E   27, 65, 66, 220
See "Financial Declaration".

Freedom   **8, 9, 10, 108,**
The absence of artificial restraint, except by laws that are gentle and moderate.   110, 124, 139,
Thus allowing us to be entirely master of our own conduct, except where essential   167
public good requires some temperate direction or restraint.

Garnishee Order
A court order to seize money from a man's bank account (or other account) to pay
a debt, such as arrears of maintenance.

Green Form
A common name for an application for limited Legal Aid.

Ground   **15-17**, 24, 32, 38,
The reason(s) given when demanding a divorce.   46-52, 158, **170,**
                                                                                   172, 177

Habeus corpus
A court order requiring a person under arrest to be brought to court, so that he
may be released, unless lawful grounds are shown for his detention.

High Court   26, 29, 31,
A court in which long or complicated divorce cases are dealt with. Appeals from   **44**, 74, 159
lower courts can go to the High Court.

Homemaker   58, 68, 69
Judges like to call a wife "the homemaker". They disregard that men are
homemakers too and usually pay for most of the home.

House of Lords   74, 118, 120
The House of Lords is the highest court in this country. It hears appeals from
lower courts. Only the European Courts are higher.

Human Rights Act 1998   73, 86, 107,
An Act made by the Westminster Parliament. It purports to implement rights and   **108**, 109, 126,
freedoms, guaranteed to the people of the United Kingdom, by the European   132, 221, 224
Convention on Human Rights.

In Chambers
"In Chambers" is a secret court. The Public and Press are kept out to conceal what
the court is doing. You should always ask for them to be admitted.

Injunction
A court order requiring someone to do something, or not do it.

Joint Property

Property held in the names of 2 or more persons.

Judgement Summons

An application to a court to have someone put in prison for not obeying a court order. This is usually only done if he ignored the court order deliberately. Committal to prison is unusual if the accused can show that it was not in his power to obey the order.

Judicial Separation (or Legal Separation)

161-3,

A Decree of Judicial Separation is a court order, issued on any of the grounds that would justify a divorce, but without the need to prove the marriage has irretrievably broken down. It means that the spouses do not have to live together, assets are divided as if there had been a divorce, but neither inherits on the death of the other. For men this usually means the seizure of their assets, without the freedom of divorce. You should avoid this.

Jurisdiction

110, 144, 151, 153, 156

The country, or territory, where a court can enforce its orders. A court also has its power limited to certain matters, for example: not all courts can deal with divorce.

Land Registry

An organisation that registers the ownership of property. A married woman can have her "interest" in her husband's property noted against his property.

Legal Aid

76, 80, 81, 84, 89, 122, 129, 133, 135, 166

Money from the Legal Services Commission to pay lawyers' bills. It is usually a loan and must be paid back after the proceedings.

Legal Aid Board

76

The Legal Aid Board is now called the Legal Services Commission (LSC).

Legal Services Commission (LSC)

76, 130, 166

The Legal Services Commission provides Legal Aid for people with low income and assets, for civil cases, including divorce.

Litigant in Person

18, 20, 95, 99, 102, 197

A person who represents himself in a court, without having his lawyer present. You are entitled to do this in all English "family" courts.

Lump Sum Order

161-2, 173, 219, 233

A court order forcing someone to make a single payment of money (usually a large amount) to someone else.

Maintenance Order

212, 240

A court order forcing someone to pay regular sums of money to someone else, usually every week or month.

Maintenance Pending Suit

161, 173

Maintenance from the time that a Petition is issued until it is decided whether there will be a divorce and financial matters are settled.

Martin Order

A court order forcing a home to be put into joint names, but for only one of them to live in it, and the property to be sold and the proceeds divided when that person moves, dies, cohabits with someone else or remarries.

Matrimonial Causes Act 1973

69, 70, 73, 104, 107, 118, 125, **158, 159,** 221

This is the main Act covering divorce in this country and seizure of assets.

Matrimonial Home

The property where a married couple live together, whether they own it or not.

McKenzie Friend

A friend, who is not a lawyer, who goes to court with someone involved in divorce proceedings. The friend can give advice to the person he is supporting, and take notes, but cannot present the case to the judge. There is nothing to prevent you from taking a journalist as your friend if you think that this might help you.

Mediation

43

Resolution of disputes, concerning divorce or separation, assisted by a third party who is not a judge. Agreement about property, money or children can be made by mutual consent.

Memorandum of Understanding

A document of matters agreed by a divorcing couple, used in mediation. It is not legally binding.

Mesher Order

A court order forcing a home to be put into joint names, but for only one of them to live in it, and the property to be sold and the proceedings divided when that person moves, cohabits with someone else, remarries or the youngest child becomes 18 and finishes full time education.

Nominal Order

84, 212, 215-6, 220

A court order for a very small amount of maintenance to be paid by one person to another (often £1 a year). This is done so that an application can be made in the future for an increase to much larger payments.

Non-Molestation Injunction
A court order prohibiting someone from assaulting someone else.

Non-resident Parent
A parent who does not live with his children, usually the father, who may be forced to pay maintenance to the mother.

Notice of Appeal   37, 72, 74,
This is a form that you complete if you decide to appeal, against a court order, to a   75, **221**
higher court. The Notice of Appeal must get to the higher court within a deadline.

Notice of Proceedings   **24**, 29
A document which comes with a divorce Petition, stating that a divorce has been
applied for.

Nullity (or Annulment)   160-163
A court order that a marriage is null and void. A divorce is then not necessary.

Occupation Order (or Ouster)   86, 87
A court order forcing someone to leave his home, or allowing someone else to live
there, or limiting a person's rights to his own home in some other way.

One-Third Rule
Forced maintenance for a wife, after divorce, where she gets one third of the
combined income, plus maintenance for any children.

Open Position   34, 35, **204**,
An offer of a financial settlement for a divorce, given in a letter, produced for a   218
court hearing on finance. A "closed position" is your fall-back position, or any
other intentions you have that you have not disclosed.

Ouster   86, 87
A court order forcing someone not to live in his own home.

Pending Suit   161, 173
Anything that happens during divorce proceedings (before a decree absolute is
issued).

Pension Sharing (or Splitting)
The value of a man's pension rights is calculated. A part is then seized and
transferred to fund a pension for his wife.

Periodical Payments Order   161, 173, 240
A court order forcing weekly or monthly payments after a divorce, for a wife or
child.

Perjury

Perjury is deliberately telling a lie in a court, or putting a lie in a document for the court. It is a criminal offence.

Personal Protection Order

A magistrate's court order preventing physical assault of a particular person.

Petition

A court document, signed by a Petitioner, asking for a divorce (and other demands).

Petitioner

The person who applies for a Petition and requests a divorce.

Pleading

Any written application or reply to a court.

Port Alert

Immigration officers at all airports and sea ports are given details of a child, to prevent him from leaving the country.

Post Nuptial Agreement (Post Marital Agreement)

A contract between a couple, when they marry, that states what each will be entitled to if they divorce. These contracts are not enforceable in the courts and are frequently ignored if they do not favour the wife.

Prayer

The formal request, in a divorce Petition, for the court orders that the Petitioner wants. She may want a divorce, her husband's home, his pension, the children and maintenance.

Pre-trial Hearing

A preliminary hearing held by a judge, with the 2 parties, to decide what information is needed, and what needs to be done, before a later hearing is held.

Prohibited Steps Order

A court order preventing a parent from doing something with a child, such as going abroad or change of name.

Property Adjustment Order

A court order transferring ownership of property, or the right to live in it, from the rightful owner to someone else. These orders are so far reaching that they can mean the complete denial of the right to personal property.

Questionnaire

A list of questions from one spouse to the other demanding information and evidence about finances.

Real Property
A home, other building, land or anything attached to such property.

Reconciliation
The decision by a couple not to divorce, to withdraw the Petition if there is one, and continue married life. (See "Conciliation".)

Recovered Assets
Any property, or other asset, stolen by one spouse from the other in a divorce.

Reply
A document from a Petitioner responding to an Answer (or cross petition) from a Respondent.

Request for Directions
An application to a court for decree nisi.

Reserved Costs
The decision on who must pay costs to be made at a later hearing.

Respondent
The defendant in divorce proceedings who has received a divorce Petition from his spouse.

Residence Order
A court order saying who a child must live with. A Residence Order is never final and you can apply for it to be changed whenever you think changing circumstances make this desirable.

Rule 2.61 Statement (or Statement of Information)
An agreed summary of finances and intentions, produced by a couple, for a court. The court is asked to approve what the couple have agreed and issue a Consent Order.

Schedule of Issues
A list of things that you and your wife disagree about, prepared for a court.

Secure Periodical Payments Order
A maintenance order forcing the payer to guarantee the payments in some way, such as providing assets large enough to secure the payments.

Secured Provision
An asset, owned by a man, seized by a court to give his wife income.

Separation Agreement
A document of matters agreed when a couple separate, usually before divorce proceedings.

Service (or Serving)
The delivery of court documents to someone in a divorce case.

Set Off
The seizure of extra assets from a man to compensate his wife for not having a pension.

Settlement
The written agreement on finances agreed by a divorcing couple, or forced by a judge.

Special Procedure
If a divorce is not contested, a decree nisi can be issued by a judge without either spouse going to court. The man's property and children can then be taken at later hearings.

Specific Issue Order
A court order giving instructions on a specific issue of a child's life.

Statement of Arrangements
A form attached to a divorce Petition giving the Petitioner's proposals for the future of children.

Statement of Information (or Rule 2.61 Statement)
An agreed summary of finances and intentions, produced by a couple, for a court. The court is asked to approve what the couple have agreed and issue a Consent Order.

Statute
A written law passed by a parliament.

Statutory Charge
Money from a divorce settlement that must go to the Legal Services Commission to repay Legal Aid.

Subpoena (or Witness Summons)
A court document requiring a person to appear as a witness at a hearing.

Summons
A document from a court requiring a person to appear or make a response.

Supervision Order
A court order requiring a local authority to supervise a child's life for a given time.

Tactical Answer, or Appeal, or Application

An Answer (to a Petition), an appeal, or an application to a court, which is made with the intention of offering to withdraw it, in return for a concession from your wife.

Tangible Property

An asset that has obvious value, such as a home or furniture.

Tenancy in Common

Joint ownership of property in which a co-habiting couple each has a distinct share.

Testimony

The evidence of a witness, under oath, for a court.

Threshold Criteria

Conditions which must apply before a court will make an order of some kind.

Transcript

A written record of what was said at a court hearing.

Trial

Examining and testing evidence at a court hearing. You may be asked to take an oath and answer questions from your wife's lawyer. Your wife, and any witnesses, may give evidence and you can question them.

Trial Bundle

A photocopy of all letters, statements and other documents for a court hearing, prepared by the Petitioner's solicitor. The judge gets a copy of this, so do you and your wife.

Trust

A legal entity, like a company, set up by a settlor, so that a trustee holds and manages assets for beneficiaries.

Ultra vires

When a court wrongly does something for which it has no lawful power.

Undertaking

A promise by a person to a court to do, or not to do, something. A court may penalize someone who does not comply with an undertaking.

Usher

A junior clerk who shows people into a court.

Wardship
A court taking control of all major decisions in a child's life.

Welfare Officer (CAFCASS Officer)
A Welfare Officer is a social worker, who works for the family courts, and reports to judges on what should happen to children when parents divorce, or separate. Welfare Officers have a bad reputation. They are feminist and heavily biased in favour of pressuring children to live with their mother.

"Without Prejudice"
These words are put at the top of a letter that is not to be shown to a judge, unless there is a dispute about who will pay costs.

Woolf Report
The Woolf Report "Access to Justice" reviewed the legal system in 1996. One of its findings was that courts must be pro-active in helping anyone who represents himself, providing direct assistance. Judges must give help to the person in presenting his case.

"**Y**ardstick of Equality"
A muddled idea by an elderly English judge. He thought that a woman should have a major share of her husband's property when she divorces him, regardless of her financial contribution to the marriage, and regardless of her behaviour.

For more than a thousand years, the English people have built the finest system of laws in the World to guarantee their rights and freedoms. This is the Common Law.
It is the most vital part of our Constitution.

This Common Law has been built not only by men of affairs, and judges, but also by the ordinary people, who contributed their ideas on fairness and justice from their towns and villages throughout the country.

The sacred principle of our ancient rights is that they may only be added to, never taken away. It has been our boast that this has given us a Constitution that is the only one in the World whose direct purpose is freedom.

It is a shameful scandal that we now have secret courts forced on us, abusing our fundamental rights to property and family life.

The Ghost of Justice

Drawing by Patricia Tucker.

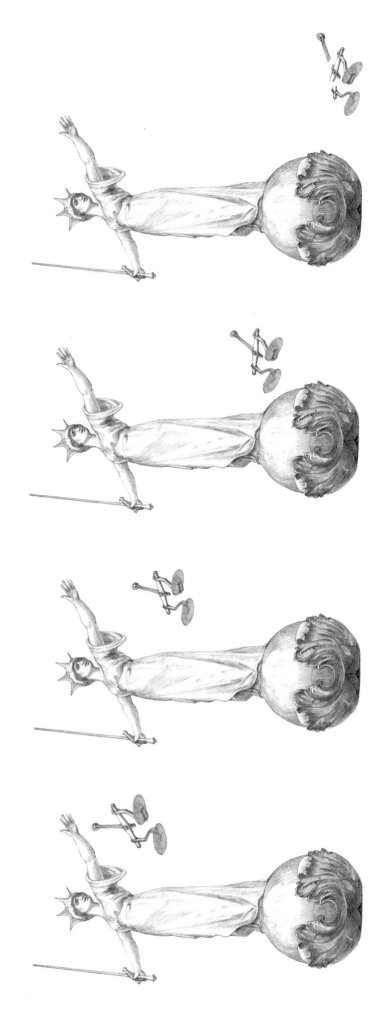

Sundridge Publishing